THE
WARRIORS
OF ANBAR

THE MARINES WHO CRUSHED AL QAEDA—
THE GREATEST UNTOLD STORY OF THE IRAQ WAR

★

ED DARACK

FOREWORD BY

COLONEL JAMES E. DONNELLAN, USMC (RET.)

Da Capo

Hachette Book Group supports the right to free expression and the value of copyright. The purpose of copyright is to encourage writers and artists to produce the creative works that enrich our culture.

The scanning, uploading, and distribution of this book without permission is a theft of the author's intellectual property. If you would like permission to use material from the book (other than for review purposes), please contact permissions@hbgusa.com. Thank you for your support of the author's rights.

Da Capo Press
Hachette Book Group
1290 Avenue of the Americas, New York, NY 10104
HachetteBooks.com
Twitter.com/HachetteBooks
Instagram.com/HachetteBooks

Printed in the United States of America

First Edition: November 2019

Published by Da Capo Press, an imprint of Perseus Books, LLC, a subsidiary of Hachette Book Group, Inc. The Da Capo Press name and logo is a trademark of the Hachette Book Group.

The Hachette Speakers Bureau provides a wide range of authors for speaking events. To find out more, go to www.hachettespeakersbureau.com or call (866) 376-6591.

The publisher is not responsible for websites (or their content) that are not owned by the publisher.

Print book interior design by Jeff Williams.

Library of Congress Cataloging-in-Publication Data has been applied for.

ISBNs: 978-0-306-92265-7 (hardcover), 978-0-306-92266-4 (ebook)

LSC-C

10 9 8 7 6 5 4 3 2 1

To the Warriors of Anbar

Notably, the Fallen of 3/3, 2/3, and Supporting Units (*):

3/3

Andres Aguilar Jr.
David Christoff
Adam Conboy
Edward Davis III
Michael Estrella
Brandon Hardy
William Leusink
Eric Lueken

Jose MarinDominguez
Ryan Miller
Lea Mills
Jason Ramseyer
David Roddy*
Yull Estrada Rodriguez
Martin Yearby
Hatak Yuka Keyu

2/3

Dustin Adkins*
Anthony Aguirre
Joshua Alonzo
Joshua Booth
Donald Brown
Timothy Brown
Daniel Chaires
James Chamroeun
Matthew Clark
Matthew Conte
James Davenport
Terry Elliott
Joseph Ellis*
Kermit Evans*
Mario Gonzalez

Derek Jones
Gary Koehler*
Charles Komppa*
Edwardo Lopez
Joseph McCloud
Jeremy Sandvick Monroe
Daniel Morris
Stephen Morris
Jennifer Parcell*
Christopher Riviere
Michael Scholl
Joshua Sticklen
Heath Warner
Jeromy West

CONTENTS

MAPS

FOREWORD

COLONEL JAMES E. DONNELLAN, USMC (RET.)

On a cold day in March 2007, I attended a meeting of the sheiks and local leaders of the Iraqi towns of Haditha, Haqlaniyah, and Barwana (the key components of a region we called the "Haditha Triad"), adjacent to the forward operating base of Echo Company. We had designed the meeting primarily to introduce our recently appointed mayor, Abdul Hakim, and the police chief, Colonel Farouk, to the local leaders to convince them that they could work with us and that our goals were more like theirs than those of Al Qaeda in Iraq (AQI). While our battalion had organized and paid for the event, our intent was for the coalition forces to play a deliberately quiet part in the meeting. I would make a few brief remarks, but we really wanted the mayor and police chief to be front and center to show the leaders of the Triad that something approaching "normal life" might be possible. We saw an opportunity to capitalize on some of the enemy's mistakes in how they treated the citizens of the Triad, and we wanted the support of these key leaders in a new initiative.

This new focus was a dramatic shift from the improvised explosive device attacks, sniper engagements, vehicle check-points, and bloodshed—from Americans, Iraqis, and foreign terrorists—that had marked the first four months of our deployment. When we arrived in the Triad in September 2006, the area had recently exploded in a level of violence not seen since the early days of the war. There was no functioning government, no reconstruction projects, and the community leaders had all gone into hiding—or were cooperating with the terrorists and insurgents. Now, we were listening to local leaders talk about hiring schoolteachers, fixing water supply problems, and repairing long-neglected streetlights. These were "normal" problems, good problems.

This is the story of one corner of the war in Iraq. It is the story of Marines, supported by service members from all branches, making progress against incredible odds. It contains inspiring examples of what our nation's young warriors are capable of—despite a mission that was politically unpopular, strategically questionable, and tactically difficult to the extreme.

I had the responsibility and privilege of leading the 2nd Battalion of the 3rd Marine Regiment ("2/3") during our earlier Afghanistan deployment in 2005–2006 and then our Iraq deployment from September 2006 to April 2007. We were fortunate to be on the ground in the Haditha Triad when the tide turned, but the changes were the result of *successive* deployments of Marine battalions, active and reserve, who waged significant fights for the Triad, often stretched incredibly thin. They had lived by the mantra that had guided Marine forces in Al Anbar since General Jim Mattis's initial guidance to 1st Marine Division: that there is "No Better Friend, No Worse Enemy" than a US Marine.

We followed an exceptional battalion into Iraq, just as we had the previous year in Afghanistan. Lieutenant Colonel (now Brigadier General) Norman "Norm" Cooling and 3/3 had gone to great lengths, detailed herein, to bring Colonel Farouk back as police chief. On Day One of our deployment, however, we nearly lost Farouk's support, due to the butchery of AQI. Over the course of the next ninety days, the Marines of 2/3 and a handful of Iraqi Police beat back the enemy from daily attacks that had averaged thirteen per day to less than one per day. We gained access to the small islands where the insurgents hid their tons of explosives and other weapons caches. Engineers built a berm around the city to help us control access through hardened checkpoints. We ran countless patrols each night, meeting the people and mapping out the community leaders. We took that fledgling police force of twenty-four Iraqis and shepherded their recruiting and training to turn over a force approaching 300 at the end of our deployment. It has been said that a necessary step of any counterinsurgency is to make the population respect you more than they fear you and the enemy fear you more than they hate you. Ultimately, that is what the Marines and sailors who fought there did.

As our meeting wrapped up, we introduced Colonel (now Lieutenant General) H. Stacy Clardy, the commanding officer of Regimental Combat Team-2, to some of the key leaders. Clardy was struck by the dramatic change in circumstances from his Pre-Deployment Site Survey (PDSS) a few months earlier and was effusive in his praise of the battalion. Just as Sergeant Major Pat Wilkinson and I had done with our own Marines, I reminded Colonel Clardy that we were just fortunate to be the "last guys to carry the ball over the line." A lot of sacrifices had been made by our predecessors who did not get to see the results. We got to see a mayor choosing to focus on issues beyond security and local shop owners actively working to rebuild their city and take it back. Children were returning to school and playing in the streets, souks were stocked full of food and other goods, and we saw people smiling and waving when we passed, instead of running inside. We could listen to questions about streetlights and water mains. These were good problems to have, indeed.

I met Ed Darack during 2/3's Afghan deployment in 2005–2006. Ed is uniquely qualified to tell this story, having walked patrol with each company of 2/3. He has met most of the squad leaders as well as platoon and company commanders. While he focuses on the most dramatic periods of our deployment, for every event covered in these pages, there are equally heroic and poignant stories left untold from across the battalion, our predecessors, and indeed across the Iraq War.

As in any combat mission, too many Marines and other service members who fought in the Triad did not return home from their deployments. Others spent years recovering from their injuries. Not a day has gone by since I left battalion command that I have not reflected on their sacrifices. I would remind the reader that the vast majority of the life and death decisions documented in these pages were made by Marines and sailors who were between the ages of eighteen and twenty-four—and all *chose* to be there, as members of an all-volunteer force. Their maturity, understanding of counterinsurgency, relentless warrior spirit, and love for their fellow Marines will continue to inspire me as long as I live. I hope it inspires you.

Portsmouth, RI
June 2019

INTRODUCTION

THE TOUGHEST, MOST BRUTAL FIGHT

IN THE LATE SUMMER OF 2006, MEMBERS OF THE 2ND BATTALION of the 3rd Marine Regiment (abbreviated "2/3" and pronounced "two-three")—the Island Warriors—said goodbye to their families, friends, and home base at Kaneohe Bay, Hawaii, and embarked on a journey to the other side of the world. Days later, they arrived at their destination: the Haditha Triad region of western Iraq. The Triad, a geographic term coined by the Marine Corps, consisted of the city of Haditha and a number of surrounding towns and villages, notably Barwana, Haqlaniyah, and Albu Hyatt. Located at a strategically critical point on the Euphrates River corridor between the Syrian border and the cities of Fallujah and Ramadi, the Triad ranked as one of the most vital locations for the group known as Al Qaeda in Iraq (AQI) and its affiliates throughout Operation Iraqi Freedom (OIF). Far from the country's large cities and surrounded by vast sweeps of desolate, uninhabited desert, Haditha and its satellite towns lay in the heart of the country's Al Anbar Province, AQI's base of operations and lifeline throughout the war.

The battalion arrived in the Triad well into the war's fourth year. Since the March 20, 2003, official kickoff of Operation Iraqi Freedom, the nature of the conflict had progressed from a blunt "shock and awe" fight to a complex, highly nuanced counterinsurgency campaign piqued by hard "kinetic" regional thrusts and smaller surgical counterterror strikes. 2/3's overarching goal for its seven-month tour: improve security for the local inhabitants of the war-ravaged Triad by decimating outside AQI influence while simultaneously supporting a resurgent local government and economy. It would continue the work of previous Marine Corps battalions that had rotated through the Triad, notably its sister battalion, the 3rd Battalion of the 3rd Marine Regiment, which 2/3 "relieved-in-place" upon its arrival in late summer 2006.

Despite steadfast progress by 3/3 and previous units, 2/3 arrived exactly at a critical moment in the war, when unforeseen circumstances created nearly insurmountable consequences. As components of the 1,100-strong battalion task force settled into their respective areas of operation throughout the region, key events, conditions, and factors coalesced to foment an enduring hurricane of adversity, violence, and calamity.

Al Qaeda in Iraq, eviscerated from blow after blow in key strongholds like Fallujah and Ramadi, fell back to the Triad, assuming the posture of a cornered, mortally wounded animal. Overlooked by global media, the region had served as a relative sanctuary where AQI could thrive and grow over the course of Operation Iraqi Freedom. But, with nowhere else to flee to and ravage, AQI transformed the Triad into a theater for its last, desperate gasps for survival just as 2/3 arrived.

Yet the terrorists of Al Qaeda in Iraq didn't lash out against the battalion in large, concerted efforts. The enemy hid among the locals they terrorized and had threatened into submission and silence. They melted into the beaten populace and under and among the shadows of the labyrinthine alleyways and back streets of the city. Then they struck—knowing that members of the battalion could rarely hit back with their traditionally overwhelming force because the Marines of 2/3 held the safety of the locals as their highest priority.

AQI attacked with sniper fire, with volleys of mortars and rockets, with tossed hand grenades, with complex ambushes from well-concealed positions, and, perhaps most insidiously, with improvised explosive devices, or IEDs—hidden bombs detonated remotely or by triggers hidden in roads, trails, even open desert ground. In its drastic attempts to derail the nascent post-invasion Iraqi government, AQI indiscriminately killed and maimed innocent local men, women, children, Iraqi national forces, and, of course, members of 2/3, who had come to fight for the Iraqi people and their country's security and growth.

Forged in the fire of recent combat, having acquired a half year of intensive, specialized training before the deployment, and led by mission-focused, dedicated officers, 2/3 immediately charged ahead with its assignment. But the circumstances proved more complex than any before experienced in the war in Iraq. The phantom enemy threw everything it had at the battalion and simultaneously sought to drive wedges between the locals and 2/3, directly, through threats and intimidation, and indirectly, through carefully coordinated information operations. The enemy proved relentless and brutal. Within the first weeks of the battalion's arrival, AQI had killed many and wounded dozens of members in horrific, bloody attacks. Further complicating the fight, 2/3's higher command, located miles distant from the Triad, hammered the battalion with burdensome restrictions that—were it not for the unrelenting drive of 2/3's senior leadership—would have crippled it to the point of defeat at the hands of the enemy.

For all members of the 2nd Battalion of the 3rd Marine Regiment, their Iraq tour would prove the toughest, most brutal fight of their lives—arguably the toughest, most brutal fight experienced in modern war. Despite the circumstances, despite the viciousness of an enemy desperately striking them and the local populace, despite the losses, despite the absolute necessity of restraint, and despite the crushing demands of their higher command, the members of the battalion would ultimately see their toil and sacrifice yield success—absolute, unmitigated victory. They accomplished this through discipline, dedication, resiliency, creativity, and classic, time-honed Marine Corps warfighting prowess: in their counterinsurgency campaign, they held protecting the locals and rebuilding the government, security forces, and economy as their highest duty.

Far beyond simply stating these intentions, their actions proved their resolve to the people of the Triad, winning their steadfast allegiance over any obedience coerced by AQI. When moments demanded caution in the face of potential harm or loss of innocent Iraqi life, they kept their trigger fingers straight. When moments demanded action, they struck swiftly and decisively. From the second they set foot in the Triad till the moment they had the area to their backs on their way home, they acted with utmost determination and fidelity to mission, to the Iraqi people, and to each other, even in the darkest of hours—and each and every member of the battalion experienced some of the bleakest, most horrifying of these moments during this tour. Their fight—unlike any other—represents one of the greatest untold stories of surmounting overwhelming adversity to achieve victory in modern war, one completely overlooked by history.

This book chronicles this incredible chapter of modern military history by weaving together the most salient and emblematic components of 2/3's deployment to the Triad through the progression of their time there—stories of bravery, sacrifice, incredible hardship, horror, and ultimate victory.

AGAINST AN ARMY OF PHANTOMS ON A BATTLEFIELD OF SHADOWS

LANCE CORPORAL MIKE SCHOLL PEERED DOWN THE BARREL OF his M240B machine gun, hyperalert, poised, and ready. Positioned in the turret atop an "up-armored" Humvee, he smoothly panned the gun left, then right, searching through the weapon's iron sights for any sign of an impending attack. His right index finger pressed arrow-straight against the 240's trigger guard, Scholl eyed each and every component of the scene before him: rows of palm trees, distant cars, divots in surrounding roads, an overgrown field to his left, a gathering of Iraqi locals a few dozen yards down the road to his right. He scanned for even the slightest out-of-place detail: an unusually large plastic bag, a tube of caulk in the middle of a road, a strange movement in a window, anything. The scene before him was still—at that instant. But Scholl knew that it could explode in raging violence in a split second, from any direction, as it had so many times before during this deployment.

The Humvee in which Scholl manned the 240 stood just fifty meters from the western shore of the Euphrates River in the

Bani Dahir neighborhood of the city of Haditha. Called and written "Bonnie-D" by Scholl and others of his platoon, the area lay just over two miles south of the heart of Haditha and proved to be one of the most violent and dangerous corners of not only the Triad but also the entire Al Anbar Province.

By that day, November 14, 2006, more than two months had elapsed since Scholl and his battalion had arrived in the Triad. And by that point in their planned seven-month deployment, AQI had killed eight members of 2/3. Four of those hailed from Scholl's company: Company E, or Echo Company. The fallen ranged in age from nineteen to twenty-three, including four who were twenty-one, Scholl's age.

Despite their youth, Scholl and other Echo Marines of his patrol that morning had arrived in Iraq with considerable experience gained in combat coupled with intense training in the run-up to their departure for Iraq. Most had deployed with 2/3 the previous year to Afghanistan for the battalion's historic tour in the rugged Hindu Kush mountains of the country's Kunar, Laghman, and Nangarhar Provinces. There, weeks-long combat operations took them through the storied mountains near the border with Pakistan on hunts for Al Qaeda, the Taliban, and other terrorists and insurgents during a long-term counterinsurgency campaign.

On the street in front of Scholl, twenty-year-old Corporal Mario Anes, who had served side by side with Scholl in Afghanistan, studied the scene at Bonnie-D. He took carefully placed step after carefully placed step, seeking any telltale signs of enemy activity. Corporal James Steuter, also a veteran of 2/3's Afghan tour, kept a close eye not only on potential enemy activity but also, like all on the patrol that morning, on others of his unit.

The day had begun for Scholl and others of his patrol just as the deployment had for the entire battalion: brutally violent from the very start. The Echo Company base, located in the heart of Haditha, regularly took fire: from mortars, from rockets, from snipers, from hand grenades, and from rocket-propelled grenades. No place in the city was safe, not even inside the wire of Echo's walled compound. "I got outside that morning to get ready and I see tracers slamming into Mike's truck," recalled Steuter. "That was how the day started—pretty much like every day to that point."

Under fire earlier that morning, Scholl had swan-dived into his truck's turret as Steuter sprinted to get into a position to identify the location of the attackers. BOOM! A rocket-propelled grenade smashed into the top of a wall near Steuter. The detonation blew a chunk of concrete onto Steuter's helmeted head. "A great start to my twenty-first birthday," he recalled. But before Steuter or Scholl could even locate the attackers, much less return fire, the ambush stopped.

The fighter—or fighters—ended their assault mere seconds after the first burst of machine gun fire. Then they dissolved into the patchwork of the dusty city of winding narrow streets, stoic concrete buildings, and a cowed and demoralized citizenry behind which AQI almost always hid after each of their attacks. Mike, Mario, James, and others of Echo Company and the entire battalion fought against an army of phantoms on a battlefield of shadows during their tour in the Triad.

Despite the daily—sometimes hourly—assaults by AQI, Scholl, Anes, Steuter, and the others of that morning's patrol never let their guard down or let the death and mayhem inflicted upon the battalion and the locals erode their resolve. Seeing such great compatriots in arms—*brothers*—die, at such young ages, and witnessing local Iraqis, including children, lose their eyesight, hearing, limbs, and lives could have broken them. But they didn't break—instead, the adversity pushed them to grow stronger, to be more resolute in their mission. Although many pondered whether they'd ever return home after witnessing the enemy's onslaught in those first weeks, all pushed ahead with an eye toward not just completing the mission but also winning. And no one ever lost sight of what they would find when they returned home. For some, like Mike Scholl, it would be a new addition to the family. Just weeks prior to the November 14 patrol in Bonnie-D, Scholl's wife, Melissa, had given birth to their daughter, Addison. He couldn't wait to return home and meet her in person. He talked about her to Anes, Steuter, and others every day.

IN THE TURRET of the Humvee, Scholl swept the gun's sights side to side, looking, focusing, listening, searching. BOOM! A hand grenade tossed from a shadowed alleyway detonated near Mario Anes and another Echo Marine, Lance Corporal William Burke. Dust rose in the air and rocks and shrapnel pocked the sides of buildings. Anes and Burke checked themselves and each other for wounds as Scholl, Steuter, and the rest of the patrol focused on the site of the explosion. Nothing. The phantom soldier had disappeared into the shadows of the battlefield.

Scholl and the others continued to scan for the assailant. They didn't notice the man less than a quarter mile to the southeast kneeling next to a rock in a small palm grove on the other side of the Euphrates. And they didn't see the man slide the rock a few inches to the side, exposing a six-volt battery topped with two "spring" terminals. Two stripped wires protruded from the earth next to the battery. The man connected one wire to a terminal, then he pressed the other to the second as he glared toward the Marines at Bonnie-D. . . .

1

— ★ —

SWIRLING WINDS

EVEN BEFORE THEY RETURNED FROM THEIR 2005–2006 AFGHAN-istan deployment, the members of 2/3 slated to remain with the battalion (Marines typically move from one unit to the next every two to four years) learned that they would head to Iraq a little more than a half year after arriving back home. As they had done in their Afghan deployment, the Island Warriors (the 2nd Battalion's home base is in Hawaii) would deploy to Iraq's Haditha Triad to relieve-in-place 3/3. Part of a long-term plan devised by senior Marine Corps leadership, this schedule pre-scribed that the three battalions of the regiment would each first participate in Operation Enduring Freedom by rotating through eastern Afghanistan for a seven-month tour. That would be fol-lowed by seven months back at their home base preparing to deploy to Iraq.

The plan sent 3/3 to Afghanistan first, in 2004, followed by 2/3, and then 1/3. The deployment cycle would repeat in the Haditha Triad, again beginning with 3/3. This rotation worked well for all three battalions in the regiment because the commands of each unit were familiar with those of the other two. Each in-country battalion shared general information and specific intelligence with its replacement battalion, helping refine organizational structure, equipping, training, and operational planning for the next-in-line battalion.

While in Afghanistan, 3/3, led by Lieutenant Colonel Norman "Norm" Cooling, paved the way for 2/3's fluid integration into the battlespace. "The structure set us up for success," stated Major Rob Scott, 2/3's executive officer, or XO, during 2/3's Afghan deployment. 2/3 similarly worked to help 1/3 as it rotated into support of Operation Enduring Freedom.

During the seven-month period between 3/3's return from Afghanistan and its departure to western Iraq, Cooling and his battalion staff sought to best align their training and operational outlook for the Triad. Although both Iraq and Afghanistan are part of US Central Command, the Triad differed starkly from eastern Afghanistan in physical geography, human geography, environmental conditions, history, enemy composition and posture, and US Department of Defense outlook. Transitioning from operating in the lofty mountains and steep terrain of the Hindu Kush near the frontier with Pakistan to the streets, alleyways, palm groves, and flat desert sweeps of the Triad would require significant operational shifts, at all battalion levels.

HADITHA, AT THE center of the Triad, lies 130 air miles west-northwest of Iraq's capital of Baghdad, in the northeastern quadrant of Al Anbar Province. Al Anbar, or just Anbar, which borders Syria on its northwest, Jordan on its western extremity, and Saudi Arabia on its southwest, ranks as the largest province in Iraq, dominating the western portion of the country, most of its extent defined by barren sweeps of flat, sun-scorched desert just a few hundred feet above sea level. The Euphrates River strikes through the province and stands as its most important geographic feature.

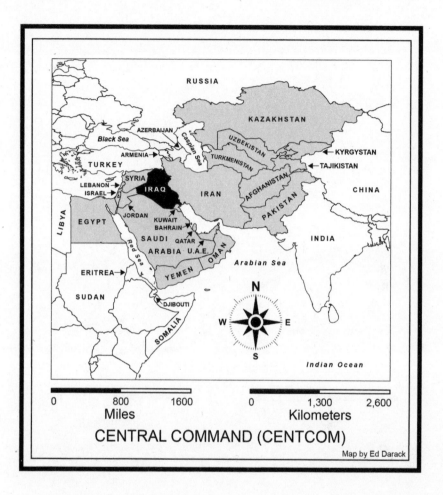

CENTRAL COMMAND (CENTCOM)

Map by Ed Darack

Haditha, population twenty-five thousand, and its satellite towns and villages would never have become settlements, much less modern population centers, but for the nourishing Euphrates. The waterway, which stretches nearly two thousand miles in length and passes through both Turkey and Syria before entering Iraq, is flanked along its length by a lush riparian zone. This "ribbon of life," fed by the Euphrates, supports agriculture and is the basis for urban development along its path. The corridor interconnects the Haditha Triad with the cities of Al Qaim and Rawa to the north, and Hit, Ramadi (the provincial capital of Al Anbar Province), and Fallujah to the south.

Map by Ed Darack

IRAQ REGIONAL

The Euphrates River corridor also served as a main artery for terrorist operations throughout Operation Iraqi Freedom. At its core, AQI was a foreign invading force, and its fighters, weapons, supplies, and money flowed into Iraq along this corridor. Cities on this route—like Haditha, Fallujah, and Ramadi—acted as natural layovers and "forward operating bases" for the organization. Both the population centers as well as the open desert adjacent to them provided training areas and places to cache weapons and supplies. Of course, the populations of the cities were themselves targets for AQI to control as the organization marched toward its goal—Baghdad.

Because the natural geography of the Euphrates River directly supported the movement of the enemy, it thus became the operational focus of US forces in Al Anbar—all eyes turned to the river. AQI, using its loose Sunni ideological affiliation, tried to make inroads with the predominantly Sunni population of the Al Anbar region in the cities and towns along the river. It also used murder, rape, threats, and other means of forcible coercion.

With the Iraqi government's focus almost wholly on the security of Baghdad, initially little thought was given to areas in the "hinterlands" of Al Anbar. But as AQI increased its activity in the cities along the Euphrates, gradually making its way toward Baghdad, the attention intensified—as did Marine Corps operations. Not only did the Marines smash AQI in Ramadi and Fallujah, but they also hit the enemy in the more northerly reaches of the Euphrates corridor, in Al Qaim and in Rawa.

While the Marine Corps racked up success after success in cities and towns along the Euphrates River, it also took hits, notably blows in the Haditha Triad, which had become an "economy

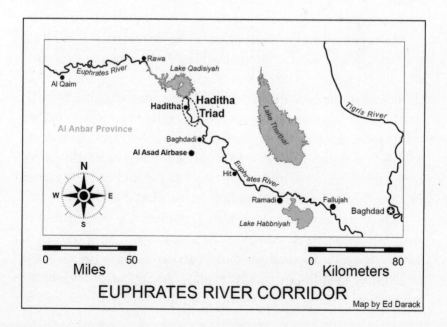

EUPHRATES RIVER CORRIDOR

Map by Ed Darack

of force" effort during the focus on Fallujah. In early March 2005, the 3rd Battalion of the 25th Marine Regiment, a Marine Corps Reserve battalion based out of Brook Park, Ohio, arrived in western Iraq and conducted operations in the Haditha Triad and in the Al Qaim region near the border with Syria.

By the time 3/25 departed Iraq, the battalion had lost forty-eight members, including two attached Navy Hospital Corpsmen (medics), the highest number of deaths suffered by a Marine Corps battalion since the October 23, 1983, Beirut bombing attack that killed over two hundred Marines and sailors of the 1st Battalion of the 8th Marine Regiment. The vast majority of 3/25's deaths occurred in the Triad, including six scouts/snipers killed on the outskirts of the city of Haditha. AQI stole their weapons and other gear and produced a number of propaganda videos.

This number also included eleven killed when a massive improvised explosive device completely obliterated an AAV-7 (an assault amphibious vehicle) on a road outside of Barwana. The blast killed a total of fifteen (including three Marines of the 4th Assault Amphibian Battalion and one Iraqi interpreter) and left only one gravely wounded survivor.

"In the years and months prior to the arrival of 3/3 and then 2/3, establishing security in the Haditha Triad area was problematic due to force cap restrictions," explained Lieutenant Colonel Ron Gridley, the executive officer of Regimental Combat Team 7, or RCT-7. Deploying for twelve-month cycles, regimental combat teams were stood up as higher commands to Marine battalions and their attachments. RCT-7 would be the higher headquarters of 3/3 for its entire seven-month tour, and would be 2/3's higher HQ for the first months of its time in the Haditha Triad.

"Once the government of Iraq saw that they needed to pay more attention to Al Anbar to fight insurgents and terrorists, they only really focused on those parts of the province closest to Baghdad—Fallujah and Ramadi," Gridley said. "While we at the RCT level saw that we needed additional resources up in the Haditha and Al Qaim areas, by law, we just couldn't get any more because of force cap restrictions—there was a predetermined, limited amount to go around and this was pre-surge, so we had to pull Marine battalions and other Marine assets away from Haditha to support efforts down in Fallujah and Ramadi. Once operations there drew to a close, then the battalions would return, but the absence always allowed the enemy enough time to regroup and get really dug in," Gridley explained.

"Once you start a counterinsurgency, you can't take a break from it. You're not just fighting against the enemy, you're fighting equally as hard, actually harder—much harder—for the trust, respect, and allegiance of the local population. If the locals see you just come and go, they're never going to align with you because when you go, the enemy comes out and tortures and executes any of the locals who helped you when you were there. We saw this a lot throughout Iraq."

Gridley noted the "clear, hold, build" maxim central to Marine Corps counterinsurgency doctrine. The initial goal, *clear,* rids an area of operations (AO) of insurgents and terrorists. Then comes *hold,* when a campaign maintains stability in a region so that forces can work with locals to *build* a government and a sustainable economy, the ultimate goal of such campaigns. "How are you going to build or rebuild *anything* if you can't hold it first? You can't. You have to maintain continuous presence till everything is stood up, including indigenous security forces that can keep the outsiders like AQI from returning," Gridley stated.

Lieutenant Colonel Cooling and his staff studied the geography, culture, and recent history of the Haditha Triad carefully during the months prior to their March 2006 deployment to the region. They would be replacing the 3rd Battalion of the 1st Marine Regiment, which, as Gridley described, had conducted counterinsurgency operations in the Triad, was then pulled to support efforts in Fallujah, and then returned. As 3/3 planned its forthcoming Iraq deployment and as 2/3 looked to the Triad on its horizon while still conducting operations in Afghanistan, two key events unfurled that would create far-reaching consequences for 3/3—and foment, directly and indirectly, two component gales of the hurricane of violence and adversity that would crash upon 2/3 when it arrived.

Although its roots and specific evolution remain uncertain—many involved claimed responsibility—a movement known as the "Anbar Awakening" surged through the Euphrates River corridor from Al Qaim, near the Syrian border, to Fallujah, just west of Baghdad. This "awakening" would play a critical role in combating the increasing enemy activity in the Haditha Triad—and would become an important factor in 2/3's mission.

Beginning in the fall of 2005, leaders of Sunni tribes along the river corridor formed alliances with Marine Corps infantry battalions and the local Iraqi security forces that the battalions trained and supported. AQI, already bloodied by hard poundings elsewhere—primarily by the Marine Corps—saw its support begin to wither and fray.

So AQI began to move its base of operations. "What remained of AQI, up and down the Euphrates, began to converge on what was their most reliable sanctuary area: Haditha," explained Captain Matt Tracy, who commanded 2/3's Echo Company, the unit to which Mike Scholl, James Steuter, Mario Anes, and William Burke belonged. Far from the Iraqi government's focus in Baghdad, and later Fallujah and Ramadi—and as such, subject to inconsistent American presence—a mortally wounded AQI began to coalesce in the Triad. "But that was just one of a number of the aspects that would make the fight so difficult for us in Haditha," Tracy noted. "There were others, one in particular."

The other component to which Tracy referred occurred in two phases, the first during the nascent stage of the Awakening, on November 19, 2005. "What it's called depends on perspective," stated a source with direct familiarity with the matter. "Some call it an 'incident,' and some call it a 'massacre,'" the source explained. As 3/3 toiled in the throes of its pre-deployment workup at the Marine Corps Air Ground Combat Center outside of Twentynine Palms, California, and as 2/3 continued its efforts in eastern Afghanistan, members of 3/1, the battalion 3/3 would be replacing, allegedly executed twenty-four unarmed Iraqi residents of Haditha.

What some called the "Haditha Massacre" and others named the more innocuous "Haditha Incident" had little immediate effect on the region—because few learned of it. With worldwide focus on Baghdad and other large cities like Fallujah and Ramadi, American and international media paid virtually no attention to Haditha and the surrounding towns and villages, despite the area's critical importance to AQI. The Marine Corps launched a thorough investigation (which, years later, culminated in just one conviction of dereliction of duty), but for months, the event cast no ripples throughout the region's population. Then, just as 3/3 arrived in the Triad in March 2006, *Time* magazine published a feature article about the event. Titled "Collateral Damage or Civilian Massacre in Haditha?" the article reverberated around the globe.

"All of the sudden everyone around the world knew about it," stated Matt Tracy. "And the enemy used it to try to convince Iraqis—namely, those in the Triad—to not trust any American. They wanted them to see all of us as the enemy, to hate us," he said. "It's important to keep in mind that there are cases after cases of AQI torturing and murdering locals to get the population to bend to their will. Countless cases. Instances that we never learned about until the locals told us," he said. "They used the media focus on it as an information tool, a long-running information operation against Marines in the region to show that the Americans were the enemy, not AQI, and this was the proof—and then all the while, they continued to behead, torture, and murder."

"It had wide-reaching ramifications for the fight for Haditha," stated a Marine Corps source familiar with the situation. "It wasn't just used against Marines in Haditha on the tactical and operational level," he said. "Anti-war politicians and others opposed to the war back home and throughout the world latched onto it to try to use it as a tool to erode support for the war effort. It became a strategic-level anti-war weapon," he said, then added: "And then AQI, in turn, used that as a tactical and operational propaganda tool to try to drive a spike between the locals of Haditha and the Americans as well as a tool directly against American troops, to demoralize them directly as well as to demoralize them by trying to show how we weren't supported back home—that people back home thought we were all cold-blooded murderers based on what was being said about us by certain politicians and media outlets."

In March 2006, as the Anbar Awakening continued to flush AQI out of Ramadi, Fallujah, and other population centers along the Euphrates River and into the Triad, 3/3 arrived in an environment increasingly hostile not from only one side, but three. "There were more members of Al Qaeda moving in. Then the article came out, stoking distrust and animosity in the locals, and then there was higher command," said a Marine Corps source intimately familiar with the situation on the ground in the Triad at that time. "There was an overreaction at the RCT level," stated a source familiar with the RCT-7 command. "There was micromanaging to begin with, but the fear of any more civilian casualties as the investigations dragged on took it levels higher. Every time a shot was fired, they opened a new investigation."

The pressure was placed most burdensomely on the squads and squad leaders, the "tip of the spear" and center of gravity of Marine Corps infantry battalions. "It was so bad that the small unit leaders felt that anything they did would result in a court martial." AQI, of course, took note of this. Although a wounded enemy, it was still fighting.

"AQI who flowed into the Triad in late 2005 through 2006 had survived Fallujah, Ramadi, and other battles. These guys survived for a reason—they were great fighters, the best, smart, and battle hardened," Ron Gridley explained. "Guys who make it that far are masters of insurgency and terror operations. They notice even the slightest changes in posture, in TTPs [tactics, techniques, and procedures], and they adjust their tactics accordingly," he said. "And they don't need to do endless Power-Points first to make their adjustments, they just make them." Further burdening 3/3, RCT-7 had the battalion divert resources to support ongoing investigations into the November 19 events. This included tracking down relatives of deceased persons, securing helicopter landing zones, and coordinating passage of outside investigators.

"Our AO was also expanded," stated Norm Cooling. As soon as the battalion arrived, the commander of RCT-7, Colonel William "Blake" Crowe, ordered 3/3 to enlarge its AO to include the city of Baghdadi, south of the Triad, a 45 percent addition in area. Encumbered by the unforeseen hurdles, 3/3 relentlessly drove ahead with its campaign. It reorganized certain components of the battalion to accommodate the multiple demands placed upon it. Despite commanding a battalion stretched thin and faced with many unanticipated obstacles over and above those directly involved with undertaking a counterinsurgency campaign, Cooling and his staff were able to quickly determine the posture of the enemy.

More importantly, they outlined a plan to defeat that enemy and give the locals the prospect of an enduring security. "With Haditha, and Al Anbar at large, there was a need to field police forces," said Cooling. "The problem with the security forces in the region at the time is that they were primarily Iraqi Army, who were mostly Shia, and outsiders. Al Anbar is Sunni, and we needed police who were Sunni, ideally from the area they'd patrol and work who knew who was an insurgent, who was cooperating with insurgents, and who would help identify insurgents and their enablers."

Previous Marine Corps battalions had built a sizable police force in Haditha, but when 3/3 arrived, none remained. When Marine forces were pulled away from the area to support combat operations in other parts of Al Anbar, AQI had moved in, captured a number of the police force, dragged them into the city's soccer field, and publicly executed them to make an example for the locals. "Others they just murdered upon finding them," Cooling explained. "The rest fled."

Haditha was a burning cauldron, and getting hotter.

2

=== ★ ===

TOWARD THE
BATTLE HANDOVER

THE NEED FOR AN INDIGENOUS POLICE FORCE IN THE HADITHA region grew more urgent with each day. With the Awakening in full swing upon 3/3's arrival, AQI flowed into Haditha. Attacks of all types increased, as did the oppressive oversight from higher up the chain of command, the restrictive rules of engagement forced on the battalion by RCT-7, and an explosion of media attention on the area following the November 2005 civilian deaths. AQI, seizing on these reports, worked to sow the seeds of distrust among the locals for the newly arrived Marines. In addition to its increasing use of violence and its propaganda campaign, AQI also began standing up a shadow government—a situation far worse than even anarchy.

3/3 held three Iraqi Police, or IP, recruitment drives during its first months in the Triad. Not a single person from Haditha or any of the surrounding areas even so much as inquired about opportunities. Al Qaeda's terror campaign was working. As the weeks and then months passed—and as enemy activity grew,

inflicting death and injury on the battalion and the locals—
Norm Cooling and his staff decided on a new tactic: if nobody
from the area would step up, perhaps the Marines could track
down previous Iraqi Police from the area who had fled to other
parts of the country. Cooling enlisted First Lieutenant Victor
"Vic" Lance, the battalion's assistant logistics officer. "Vic impressed me early as someone who understood the operational
effects we were trying to achieve in the Triad and as someone
with unusual persistence," said Cooling, who always emphasized Lance's character.

Once tasked with the project, Lance immediately began
poring over intelligence reports to identify any possible living
former Iraqi Police officer from the area. Part of his research
brought him into contact with ODA-185 (Operational Detachment Alpha 185, a unit of US Army Special Forces). Members
of ODA-185, who also worked out of the Haditha area, introduced Lance to one of their sources, "Captain Mohammad."
Captain Mohammad was a former member of the Iraqi Police
in Haditha who had fled to northern Iraq but who would occasionally venture to Haditha to visit family. Captain Mohammad told Lance of a group of men living a few hundred miles to
the north of Haditha in a village called Ash Sharqat who might
be convinced to come to the city and join the local police. The
group was led by a former Iraqi Army officer from Ash Sharqat named "Colonel Maree," who had ties to the Haditha area.
Captain Mohammad struck Lance as a bit vague but convinc-
ing enough. The young lieutenant immediately began planning
a mission to meet Colonel Maree to see whether a police force
could finally be rebuilt in the terror-plagued Triad.

"ODA-192 out of Kirkuk agreed to host our initial meeting,
which took place on June 11, 2006," Lance explained. The other
group of Special Forces personnel he speaks of were based farther to the north, in the city of Kirkuk, near Ash Sharqat. "This
first meeting was a success, as we were able to screen Maree and

a few of his closest officers." Maree further pledged his commitment to serve as the district police chief of Haditha.

Soon after that first meeting, however, the process ran into some friction. Colonel Maree organized a recruitment drive of men from Ash Sharqat, stating that at least thirty-five would step forward. "Despite our best efforts, only seven men showed up to this screening, of which only five ultimately were qualified. Colonel Maree failed his initial test, and therefore this entire plan was now in jeopardy," Lance said.

That initial setback, however, flipped to a positive note—a very positive note that would prove to be a long-term, eminently vital component of 2/3's deployment, which was, at that point, just a few months away. "While this screening initially appeared to be a failure, it was in fact an incredibly pivotal event for us, as I would come to find that one of the seven men that showed up for the screening was named Tayeh Hardan Farouk, *the former Haditha police chief*," Lance recalled. "This was the man we had been looking for since we got into theater," he said. "This was a game-changer."

Farouk—Colonel Farouk—had been an officer in the Iraqi Army for seventeen years, from 1986 to 2003. After retiring from the Army, he had returned home to Haditha to assume the position of Haditha police chief. That lasted only until the following year, when Al Qaeda descended upon the area in force and massacred the police and a number of other locals who had helped American forces, which had been pulled away from Haditha to aid with operations in other portions of Anbar. Now he had another chance to serve the people of Haditha. "Colonel Farouk didn't want to come back to Haditha to simply get a paycheck," Lance said. "Many of his former policemen, friends, and family had been killed and terrorized by Al Qaeda, and he was determined to return to his hometown to rid it of terrorists and create long-term stability. He saw me as an opportunity to do just that, and did not want to see our efforts fail."

A number of other meetings and recruitment drives ensued in the following weeks. By late August, Colonel Farouk had more than two hundred men registered. They would be the "seed" of the Haditha Police—with the plan to then recruit locally to continue building the force throughout the Triad.

As the recruits trained at the Baghdad Police Academy, Lance worked directly with Colonel Farouk and three of his most trusted IP officers to begin a carefully coordinated process of identifying AQI operatives and their supporters within Haditha. "During our first week back in the Triad, Lieutenant Colonel Cooling and I escorted Farouk around to a number of the top local leaders (mainly sheiks), and most seemed very happy to see him," Lance recalled.

Farouk and his men worked closely with the Marines of 3/3 to share valuable information on the local populace to identify terrorists. "In our first ten days [back] in the Triad, we conducted nightly targeted detentions out of each Marine FOB [forward operating base] that resulted in the arrest of over seventy members of AQI."

The locals were thrilled with Colonel Farouk's return. "City council members who were supporting Al Qaeda decided to leave town immediately. The mayor of Haditha, Emad Jawad, actually fled, as well, shortly after we brought Colonel Farouk to meet with him."

Soon the AQI shadow government began to collapse. But the terrorist group—its ranks swelling in Haditha—lashed back viciously, fighting for its very survival. "It was clear that Al Qaeda saw Farouk and his force as a major threat to their objectives in the Triad," Lance recalled. AQI ambushed patrols in which Farouk took part using improvised explosive devices. Even more telling was the terrorist group's use of accurate, extremely powerful 120mm mortars. "In short order, the location of the new police headquarters in Haditha was being targeted on a regular basis by 120mm mortars, which up to that point in our deployment we hadn't seen before," Lance said.

As 3/3 CONTINUED to conduct combat operations throughout the Triad and worked with Farouk to stand up the nascent Haditha police force, 2/3 finalized its pre-deployment training and readied to depart for Iraq. The 2nd Battalion, led by Lieutenant Colonel James "Jim" Donnellan, had been carefully studying the progress of 3/3 since its March arrival. Donnellan and his staff closely analyzed after-action reports and enemy tactics, techniques, and procedures, and researched key personnel with whom 3/3 had forged alliances. They took careful note of all recommendations made by Cooling, his battalion staff, and those of the individual company commanders in the battalion.

In the weeks leading up to the arrival of 2/3's Advanced Echelon, or ADVON (the battalion's advance party that helps pave the way for the arrival of the unit's main element), Donnellan and Cooling communicated with one another regularly. With an eye on ever-increasing security in the Triad, Cooling identified a key point. "Norm made it crystal clear that the city of Haditha was the center of gravity in the Triad," Donnellan said. "That part of the AO would require my strongest company commander." Cooling elaborated: "Haditha was the seat of Iraqi government in the area. It's where the 'city hall' was located and where the police force was headquartered," he explained. "Although not always the most volatile area in the Triad (Haqlaniyah had just as much insurgent activity), Haditha is where the insurgents focused their influence efforts."

Cooling also noted the importance of the Marines maintaining oversight of Farouk and his police force, thinking that the chief and some of his officers might use their positions to exact revenge on some of the local populace if they believed these people in any way had collaborated with AQI. "The commander in Haditha needed to be able to discern between legitimate COIN [counterinsurgency] actions and retribution or intertribal competition/conflict."

Donnellan, who had led 2/3 on its successful tour in Afghanistan, had a strong pool of leadership talent from which to choose. Captains Matt Tracy, Pete Capuzzi, and Perry Waters, the commanders of Company E, Weapons Company, and Company G, respectively, all participated in the Afghan deployment with 2/3. Captain Lance Davis, commander of Company F, did not, but was a strong leader nonetheless.

"Tracy and I fed off of each other," Donnellan said. "He just got it. He got the mission. He is just so well read; he has what General [James] Mattis calls the 'three-thousand-year-old mind.'" It was not a choice of who was "better" but of who was "most appropriate." The decision proved straightforward enough: Echo Company, led by Tracy, would take the city of Haditha as its company AO. Company G, or Golf Company, led by Waters, would take Haqlaniyah, just to the south of Haditha, and Company F, or Fox Company, led by Captain Davis, would take Barwana, across the Euphrates from Haditha. Weapons Company, led by Pete Capuzzi, would establish itself to the south of Haqlaniyah, initially at Baghdadi, and then later at Albu Hyatt, closer to Haditha, Haqlaniyah, and Barwana.

In the month leading up to the RIP/TOA, or "relief-in-place/transfer of authority" (the formal term of one military unit replacing another on site, also known as a "battle handover"), Matt Tracy built a strong rapport with Captain Andrew Lynch, the commanding officer of 3/3's India Company, in charge of the Haditha city AO for the 3rd Battalion.

Lynch explained the specifics of India Company's operations to Tracy, including how it structured the platoons, worked with Farouk and the budding Haditha police force, collaborated with the Iraqi Army forces in the area, and developed and structured its operations and operational cycles. "We built our plans each day and deployed outside the wire and worked with the IA [Iraqi Army] and met with the populace and did sweeps for weapons caches," Lynch said. "Then at night we'd go and meet with regional leaders. There were five sheiks in Haditha, and some were more aligned with us than others. I'd try to make contact with them at least once a week, and build relations with

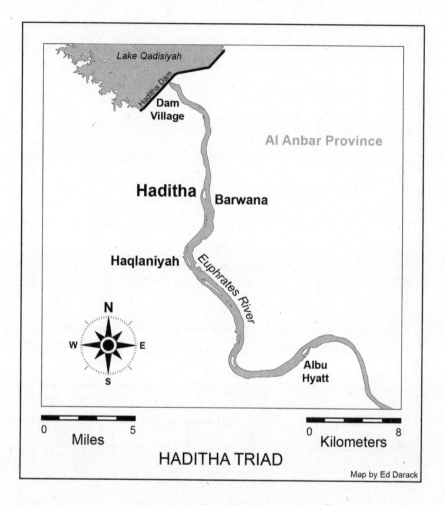

HADITHA TRIAD

Map by Ed Darack

those guys. It was typical COIN." Lynch would then combine information he gleaned from the nighttime "meet-and-greets" with that from other intelligence sources, including Farouk, to put together "raid packages" to "roll up" identified AQI operatives. It was a model that Captain Tracy and Echo Company would adopt—and refine with the help of Farouk.

As the RIP/TOA approached, the increase in enemy activity surged. "There was a confluence," Lynch said. "It really started to tip the battlespace in a negative way." Lynch explained how the successes of recent operations in other parts of the Euphrates

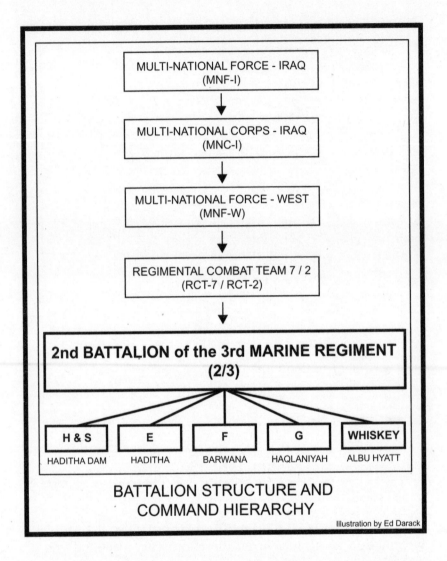

MULTI-NATIONAL FORCE - IRAQ
(MNF-I)

MULTI-NATIONAL CORPS - IRAQ
(MNC-I)

MULTI-NATIONAL FORCE - WEST
(MNF-W)

REGIMENTAL COMBAT TEAM 7 / 2
(RCT-7 / RCT-2)

**2nd BATTALION of the 3rd MARINE REGIMENT
(2/3)**

H & S	E	F	G	WHISKEY
HADITHA DAM	HADITHA	BARWANA	HAQLANIYAH	ALBU HYATT

BATTALION STRUCTURE AND
COMMAND HIERARCHY

Illustration by Ed Darack

THIS ILLUSTRATION DEPICTS the basic structure of the 2nd Battalion of the 3rd Marine Regiment and the command hierarchy under which the battalion operated during their 2006–2007 Haditha Triad deployment.

Multi-National Force—Iraq (MNF-I) ranked as the highest military command in the country and directed nationwide strategy for all coalition forces. The Multi-National Corps—Iraq (MNC-I), directly subordinate to MNF-I, oversaw nationwide military operational objectives. Multi-National Force—West (MNF-W) was a regional command that operated under

MNC-I and was responsible for an area composed almost entirely of Al Anbar Province of western Iraq. During its existence, MNF-W was commanded alternately by I Marine Expeditionary Force (I MEF) and II Marine Expeditionary Force (II MEF), each rotating leadership every 12 months. Regimental Combat Team 7 (RCT-7), a command component of MNF-W, was the direct higher command to the 2nd Battalion of the 3rd Marine Regiment (2/3) during the first half of the battalion's deployment. Regimental Combat Team 2 (RCT-2) stood as the higher command to 2/3 during the second half of the battalion's deployment. Based out of Al Asad Airbase and led by a Marine Corps regimental command staff, each regimental combat team served for 12 months and commanded a swath of terrain identified as Area of Operation Denver, which included a large portion of Al Anbar Province.

2/3 modified their organizational structure to best suit the needs of the counterinsurgency campaign that they waged in the Haditha Triad. A typical deployed battalion consists of three rifle companies (E, G, and F Companies in the case of 2/3), a Headquarters and Services ("H and S") company, and a weapons company. For their Haditha Triad deployment, 2/3 restructured their weapons company to operate as a fourth rifle company (called "Whiskey Company").

Battalion leadership based H and S out of the Haditha Dam, Company E ("Echo") out of the city of Haditha, Company F ("Fox") out of Barwana, Company G ("Golf") out of Haqlaniyah, and Whiskey Company initially out of Baghdadi, then Albu Hyatt (for the majority of the deployment), and at the K3 oil pumping facility for the final month of the battalion's tour.

The normal rifle company structure of three rifle platoons and one weapons platoon was similarly adjusted to gain a fourth maneuver platoon. Platoons were organized into three rifle squads, with each squad composed of three fire teams, and each fire team consisting of four Marines (three fire team members and one fire team leader).

Marines and sailors who hailed from a number of units outside of 2/3 were attached to the battalion for their deployment, including additional Navy Hospital Corpsmen (medical personnel), a Marine Tank Platoon, Marine Combat Engineers, Navy "Seabees" (construction battalions), and others. In total, the battalion consisted of over 1,200 personnel for the Haditha Triad deployment.

River corridor, namely, in Ramadi, "squirted" the very best, most tenacious members of AQI into the Triad. "By the end of summer, just as 2/3 arrived, Al Qaeda went from their B Team to their A Team," he said. "During most of our deployment, we'd very sporadically get hit with 82mm mortars. Then all of the sudden we're getting effective fires from 120mm mortars—daily, and inside the wire of our FOB. So, obviously, this was their pro crew," he recalled. "Then we started seeing accurate sniper fire and complex ambushes that we'd never seen before."

Each day closer to 2/3's arrival grew worse, more dire. "It was tough, trying to get through each day with conditions getting worse and worse as more and more of these fighters flowed in—and as we fought to get more people to join Farouk's crew," Lynch said. "Near the end of the summer, as we were preparing to head back, you could see how tough it was on the Marines. It was so close they [could] smell it," he said. "But nobody ever fell back onto complacency. All the Marines kept going right up to the end of the deployment." 3/3's Lima Company, charged with the Barwana portion of the Triad, lost two Marines in the final two weeks of the deployment. In all, 3/3 lost fourteen members of the battalion.

Complicating the influx of outside fighters, RCT-7's commanding officer, Colonel Crowe, who was under tremendous pressure from his higher command for a variety of reasons, began a series of investigations into a number of incidents deemed by other officers in the AO to be minor, and continued with this trend once 2/3 arrived. "Crowe directed that every incident be investigated, it seemed," recalled Ron Gridley, the executive officer of RCT-7, who worked directly for Crowe. "We were sending investigating officers out to talk with service members who had just lost a buddy. In a couple cases Crowe would personally start to interrogate guys in the Triage/Emergency Room at Al Asad [the large air base where RCT-7 was headquartered, south of the Haditha Triad]. I was livid," he said. "It seemed like he was second-guessing everyone—battalion commanders, company commanders, even squad leaders and fire team leaders. Even individual nineteen- and twenty-year-old Marines—every time they squeezed the trigger, they felt like they were getting it from both ends—from Al Qaeda, and then from the Marine Corps."

As bad as the situation became by the end of the summer of 2006, however, it would just get worse, much worse—just as the main element of 2/3 arrived.

3

★

THE EXPLODING STORM

"It wasn't hell," said Lance Corporal Max Draper, a machine gunner with Echo Company, about his first impression of Haditha. "It was worse than hell. I know it sounds cliché, but nothing could be that bad. It was beyond my worst, most horrific nightmares."

"People talk about the surge in Iraq," said Corporal James Steuter of Echo Company. "And they're talking about the surge of American forces in 2007. We got there during *Al Qaeda's surge*—that nobody talks about—which took place in Haditha. It was their last stand," he said. "They threw everything at us. What we saw and experienced—*nobody* should ever see or experience."

"We flew into Haditha Dam [area] on helicopters, and then we were supposed to get picked up by Humvees to go out to the FOBs," remembered Corporal Festus McDonough, a radio operator for the battalion. "We got there and they came out and told us that the convoy isn't coming. The convoy got blown up by a massive IED on their way to get us," he recalled. "That was [our] introduction to the deployment."

"When we first got there," recalled Lance Corporal Travis Zabroski, an infantryman with Echo Company, "I remember looking over the dam before we were mounting up for the first patrol down to Haditha. [There were] a couple firefights going on—then a couple huge IED explosions, and I remember thinking: *we're about to walk into it now—I hope we walk out of it.*"

WEEKS AFTER 2/3's ADVON arrived in the Triad, the battalion's main body departed for Iraq in three waves, between the twelfth and fourteenth of September. The majority of 2/3 passed through Al Asad Airbase, a sprawling military complex built in the 1980s by the Saddam Hussein regime and occupied by American and coalition forces in 2003 after the invasion. Home to RCT-7 (and then RCT-2), the base lies twenty physical miles south of Haditha—but worlds away from the intensity of "the fight" in the Triad.

Once the battalion arrived at Al Asad, Marine Corps CH-53D "Sea Stallion" and CH-53E "Super Stallion" heavy lift helicopters shuttled members through the skies over the Euphrates River corridor to where most of 2/3 took their first steps onto the Triad at the Haditha Dam. Built between 1977 and 1987, the massive structure, located five miles north of the city of Haditha, served as the official headquarters of 2/3, as it did for 3/3. Apart from impressive views of miles of concrete and thousands of acres of held-back water of Lake Qadisiyah, the dam grants a sweeping vista of the entirety of the Triad.

After those first impressions—many of which were accompanied by scenes of violence—members of each respective company in the battalion settled into their areas of operation in the Triad. Each company completed its "left seat, right seat" operations with those of 3/3, learning the lay of the region, individual neighborhoods, buildings, streets, even expressions to look for when passing by locals. "We'd hear 'that's an area where the enemy often hides,'" said James Steuter of this period of transition in the city of Haditha. "Captain Tracy always had a great immediate response."

"We're going everywhere, especially where the enemy hides," Tracy told his Marines during those first days. "We're going to completely dominate the entire battlespace."

As the newly arrived Marines took in their first impressions of the region, many felt they had landed in an odd, dark quasi-ghost town. "Stores and schools were closed, streets were often empty, nothing really going on," Steuter said. "It was a city. There were inhabitants, we knew there was stuff going on, but we just couldn't see or know what. If there were locals outside, they'd scatter as we approached." The mood and the atmosphere struck all of them as leaden, foreboding, constantly as if an attack was imminent, and always as if people were watching—maybe enemy, maybe friend to the enemy, maybe someone who didn't care. "It was like death was always hanging over us," Steuter said. "The air seemed tainted this strange yellowish color, the color of death waiting for us."

The official turnover of authority over the battlespace came on September 24, 2006. The last of 3/3 departed and the entire Triad was, at that point, "owned" by 2/3. All five of the battalion's companies were in place: Headquarters & Services at the Haditha Dam; Echo Company in Haditha; Fox Company in Barwana; Golf in Haqlaniyah; and Whiskey in Baghdadi, near Al Asad. The battalion command had reorganized Weapons Company into "Whiskey" to operate as a more traditional "line" company, like Echo, Fox, and Golf, but to be primarily mobile, because its part of the Triad was much larger than that of other companies and required service members to move much longer distances to visit different parts of their region. A number of other Marine Corps units attached to the battalion and came under 2/3's command. These included a platoon of tanks, the Dam Security Unit that used armed boats to patrol Lake Qadisiyah and the Euphrates, and a platoon from an Assault Amphibian Battalion (which operates assault amphibious vehicles, or AAVs). The assault amphibian platoon did not use AAVs during its time in the Triad; instead, it provided general support. Other personnel included EOD units, or explosive ordnance disposal units, and Naval Construction Battalions, or "Seabees," and Marine Corps Combat Engineers.

"Coincidentally, the twenty-fourth of September also marked the beginning of Ramadan," said Lieutenant Colonel Jim Donnellan. "And AQI knew that we were new to the area." New faces and slightly different uniform appearances gave Al Qaeda the cue that a new battalion had arrived—a time when the enemy could pounce to attempt to throw off the arriving forces before they got their footing. Furthermore, AQI, which did not have any information about 2/3 coming to replace 3/3, had been planning a campaign in the region to coincide with the start of Ramadan: the 2006 Ramadan Offensive. Although more a call to arms to the myriad AQI operatives throughout the Anbar Province than a tightly organized and coordinated operation, the offensive was one more component of the rapidly exploding storm the members of the battalion would face. Overnight, attacks on 2/3 more than tripled with the start of the Muslim observance.

On that first day of Ramadan, a Headquarters & Services company resupply convoy bound for Haditha struck an IED. The blast catapulted a Marine from a large "seven-ton" truck (officially called a Medium Tactical Vehicle Replacement, or MTVR), dislocating his shoulder, and peppered the leg of another Marine with shrapnel. The blast left both of them with concussions. The vehicles, escorted by two M1A1 Abrams tanks, halted, and Marines of the convoy—weapons ready—scanned the area for any sign of the trigger person and other hidden explosives. CRACK! CRACK! CRACK! CRACK! A number of Al Qaeda fighters, concealed in houses roughly fifty meters to their rear, opened up on them with AK-47s. A Marine machine gunner manning a .50 caliber M2 heavy machine gun mounted atop a seven-ton fired three bursts toward the attackers—but they slipped away in the shadows of the houses.

Soon after the convoy attack, AQI struck a "mounted" (vehicle-borne) Echo Company patrol in Haditha with a burst of machine gun fire. But similar to the IED strike and ambush, the attackers disappeared into the labyrinth of the city in seconds.

Around the same time, in Barwana the tire of a Fox Company truck drove over a hidden pressure-plate trigger system, detonating the explosive. BOOM! The blast of the massive IED detonation reverberated throughout the region.

A Golf Company Marine, standing post at his FOB in Haqlaniyah, just over one mile from the location of the IED strike, moved briefly outside the confines of his reinforced guard tower. CRACK! A sniper's bullet tore into his helmet just as a number of AQI fighters carrying AK-47s converged on the FOB. The bullet didn't kill him—the Kevlar helmet deflected it just enough so that it only lacerated his scalp. Golf Company Marines sprinted to his aid and then went "guns out" searching for the approaching fighters. The attackers, however, saw the Marines and fled, as did the sniper.

Back in Barwana, the Marines of the stricken Fox Company convoy jumped out of their vehicles to look for secondary IEDs. CRACK! CRACK! Gunfire pierced the ground as soon as their boots hit the pavement. An AQI fighter, sitting atop a motorcycle a quarter mile to their north, unloaded a magazine's worth of rounds from his AK-47. The Marines "sent rounds downrange" back at him, but the man tore off into the distance.

Then another lone AQI fighter opened up on another Fox Company patrol in another part of Barwana, unloading two magazines' worth of AK-47 rounds, striking one of the Marines of the patrol as he and others returned fire. The ambusher melted into the urban backdrop.

"Corpsman up!" one of the grunts of the patrol yelled when he saw his fellow Marine hit the ground, wounded. The corpsman assessed and treated his injuries. "He needs a medevac," he shouted when he saw the severity of the wound.

The patrol called for a "Dustoff"—an Army UH-60 Black Hawk air ambulance. Located twenty miles to the south at Al Asad, the Dustoff crew spun up one of their Hawks and was en route within minutes. Dustoff units—the call sign dates to the Vietnam War era—perform some of the most important, and dangerous, missions in combat: rescuing injured personnel— injured Americans, injured coalition partner forces, injured Iraqi security forces, and even injured enemy fighters.

As the Army Dustoff raced toward Barwana, another CRACK! CRACK! CRACK! rang out. AQI attacked yet another Fox Company patrol. The bursts of machine gun fire injured one. Another "Corpsman up!" shout came as another Marine fell to the ground. "Dustoff!" The attackers ran off as the Marines fired back.

Then another BOOM! An explosion ripped open the earth under a vehicle in Haqlaniyah when an EOD patrol struck an IED pressure plate. The blast injured nobody and caused only minor damage.

Throughout the entire area of operation, from near the dam in the north to Baghdadi in the south, AQI struck nonstop with IEDs, sniper fire, mortar fire, and complex ambushes—day and night.

The attacks tore up the battalion, but the Marines never slowed. "You couldn't even go outside, even poke your head outside the building, without all of your gear on," James Steuter said. "There were mortars landing inside the wire at all times of day and night." As 3/3's Captain Lynch had noted, AQI had their A Team in place—and, as Steuter remarked, they threw everything they could at 2/3.

The battalion's first loss came just two days after the official turnover and the start of AQI's Ramadan Offensive, on September 26. Haqlaniyah, the town just south of Haditha, presented snipers with a broad array of locations to hide, wait, watch—and then strike. Two days earlier, a sniper fired on Marines, but without a kill. The AQI sniper shot taken on the twenty-sixth had a different outcome and demonstrated the enemy's level of skill.

"Private First Class Christopher Riviere had been standing post at the company FOB," recalled 2/3's sergeant major, Patrick Wilkinson. "Due to the threat posed at the location by sniper fire, 3/3 had placed ballistic glass from old Humvees at the guard posts. But the sniper shot through a small gap between two of the plates—not even an inch wide—and struck Riviere, killing him." It was PFC Riviere's twenty-first birthday.

AQI inflicted the second loss for the battalion two days later, when radio operator Lance Corporal James Chamroeun, twenty, of Headquarters & Services Company, succumbed to his injuries from an IED attack.

The exploding storm had crashed down upon 2/3, and it showed no signs of mercy or abatement. AQI's attacks on the Marines did not represent all of the adversity the battalion would face, however. There was, of course, the looming presence of Colonel Crowe. And there were also the ever-present unforeseen elements.

Within the first minutes of 2/3 taking ownership of the battlespace, AQI began a relentless attack that appeared likely to crush one of the key efforts the battalion sought to achieve.

4

★

OVER BEFORE IT EVEN REALLY BEGAN?

"You need to get down here right now, sir." First Lieutenant Nic Guyton radioed Captain Matt Tracy from Echo's forward operating base in Haditha in the early afternoon of September 24. Guyton, who participated in 2/3's Afghan deployment, was one of Echo's platoon commanders and the company's executive officer.

"What's going on?" Captain Tracy asked from atop the Haditha Dam. He had just participated in the ceremony in which 3/3 officially passed control of the AO to 2/3.

"It's Colonel Farouk, sir," Guyton said calmly over the din of men screaming and wailing. "He's losing it. He and a bunch of his officers are pulling their hair out," Guyton said. "AQI interdicted the IPs and their families coming back from Ash Sharqat."

Guyton paused for a fraction of a second, enabling Tracy to ponder the very worst eventuality he could imagine. "They massacred all the men, twelve IPs total," Guyton said. "One of the wives on scene is on a sat[ellite] phone with Marwan right now. It's pandemonium here. Absolute pandemonium." Marwan, one of Echo Company's interpreters, tearfully screamed to the others in the room what the woman was describing to him. The picture she painted was beyond horrific.

Colonel Farouk had given twelve of his IPs a short leave to move their families from Ash Sharqat to Haditha, their new home. Somebody, however, leaked the plan to Al Qaeda. After forcibly stopping the caravan at a road block concealed by a blind curve, they tortured the officers in front of their wives and children. After beheading the men and mutilating their bodies, they beat and raped the women and children, but didn't kill them. They wanted the survivors to deliver a message to other civilians of Haditha: this fate will befall anyone who cooperates with the Americans.

The AQI attackers then absconded into the desert, leaving all the lifeless, desecrated bodies of the IP crumpled on the desert ground—except one: that of Colonel Farouk's youngest brother, which they took. The brutal attack delivered the perpetrators' message of terror, making a direct point to the leader of what AQI saw as its greatest enduring threat, a successful police force in the region.

Tracy's convoy roared toward the Echo FOB as the entire AO exploded in violence. The captain wondered what might become of his campaign. *Just minutes into having the battlespace formally handed to us,* he thought. *And this . . .* He knew that Farouk's reaction might destroy his plans before they even started. *Would Farouk be able to act with restraint, or would he just react in blood-chilling vengeance?*

Captain Tracy had met Farouk in person for the first time only weeks earlier. The two were introduced during the ADVON period, when Tracy accompanied Lieutenant Colonel Donnellan, Lieutenant Colonel Cooling, Captain Lynch, and Colonel Farouk to a meet-and-greet out in the "'ville," as Tracy would come to know Haditha. The purpose of the meeting was to introduce Tracy and Donnellan to the remaining members of the city council—all two of them. But they didn't show. The two remained locked away safely in their homes, cowering in fear for their lives over being seen with Farouk and the Marines. So, Farouk had some of his IPs arrest the council members and drag them to the meeting. As they waited, Tracy and Donnellan spoke with Farouk and learned firsthand his hatred of the enemy.

Stern and square-jawed, Farouk stared intensely at each Marine as he conversed with him. They learned of Farouk's history in Haditha—a history slashed by losses suffered at the hands of Al Qaeda. Members of the group had killed dozens of his family members, friends, and fellow IP—often torturing and beheading them. AQI had then displayed their decapitated, naked corpses in the most conspicuous locations in the city: at the soccer field, at major intersections, hung from power poles.

Tracy and Donnellan realized that revenge likely drove Farouk more than innate compulsion for civic service and duty, but each concluded that, in that tumultuous time, he was the ideal person for the job. Farouk impressed each as thoroughly tough, driven, and persistent. He had faithfully served Saddam Hussein in the way that Saddam Hussein had ruled: with an iron fist.

As such, Donnellan and Tracy believed that they could "employ" Farouk—but only with close oversight. Farouk clearly strove to win, seemingly at all costs, and that resonated with Tracy. During their first meeting, the captain unequivocally decided that Farouk would indeed be the critical factor in winning the city. At that meeting, Captain Tracy committed to using the colonel and his IP to accomplish the battalion's mission. Haditha was the battalion's main effort, and Colonel Farouk would be Tracy's central pillar.

Racing through the dusty streets toward the Echo forward operating base—all on the convoy prepared to hit an IED or "take contact" from machine gun bursts or rocket-propelled grenades (RPGs)—Captain Tracy readied himself to face Farouk.

Minutes later, Tracy walked into the base's combat operations center, or COC.

"My family is disavowing me!" Farouk roared as Tracy calmly walked toward the police chief. "Twelve of my men are dead! I have to go back to Ash Sharqat!" Farouk screamed. "This is not working. I only have twelve police officers remaining!"

The other two hundred that he had originally recruited with Vic Lance continued their training at the Baghdad Police Academy. "They'll learn of this and never come to Haditha!"

Tracy stared at Farouk as the other IP officers, clad in dark blue uniforms, continued to wail in sorrow and agony at the loss.

"You know that the head of AQI is right here in Haditha?" Farouk said.

A squad of Marines outside the COC was preparing to embark on a foot patrol. With a last look at Farouk, Tracy turned and lunged out of the room.

"Carson, wait!" he barked to Corporal Nic Carson, the squad's leader. "Don't step yet. There might be a change of plans. In fact, I'm pretty sure there will be a change of plans."

Tracy jumped back into the COC and faced Farouk. "Did you just say that THE HEAD of AQI is right here?" he asked, then paused. "IN HADITHA?"

Corporal Carson walked into the room. "Sir," Carson said, during the brief lull in the conversation.

"Yeah, corporal."

"What are we doing?"

Tracy eyed Carson for a split second. "Stand by, corporal." The captain turned back and stared at Farouk.

"The person who did this is right here, right here in Haditha," Farouk said.

"The head of all of Al Qaeda in Iraq," Tracy spoke slowly. "Right here, in Haditha?"

"The head of Al Qaeda. Right here!" Farouk yelled. "In Haditha! I've wanted to get him since I've been here!"

"Carson!"

"Yes, sir."

"Your plans *have* changed," Tracy said in his typically calm but penetrating tone. "We're going to go out and get the head of Al Qaeda in Iraq. Let everyone in the squad know."

"Uh, yes, sir," Carson responded. "Yes—uh—sir."

"You and your men meet us at the Mouse Hole in ten minutes," Tracy said to Farouk. "Me and you—right now, we're gonna get this guy."

"What?" Farouk said, looking around the COC. "You're not going to have to ask permission? You're not going to have to make a PowerPoint? You're not going to have to wait two or three days while your command in Al Asad gives you an answer—and then says no because they're worried about hurting an innocent bystander?"

"Right now," Tracy said. "Right now. Meet me at the Mouse Hole in ten minutes." Tracy looked over at Corporal Carson. "Let's get to the Mouse Hole."

"Let's move!" Carson commanded. "Everyone stage up at the Mouse Hole!" The Mouse Hole, a four-foot-diameter, roughly circular opening bashed with a sledge hammer through the wall separating the FOB from the city, allowed a relatively low-profile means of entry and exit to the streets of Haditha.

"This won't be the usual seventy-two-hour approval process to put together a raid package, corporal," Tracy said to Carson. "Ten minutes," he said. "Here we go."

The squad readied their weapons and double-checked their protective gear. Five minutes later, Farouk and his men arrived at the Mouse Hole armed with holstered 9mm pistols and baseball bats. The police chief led his officers and the squad of Marines to a compound just a minute's walk from the Mouse Hole.

"This is it," Farouk said. "This is where the guy stays." The IPs under his command bashed out the windows of the compound with their bats, then yelled for all in the home to come out. Nobody emerged, however. Then they smashed open the front door of the compound, drew their guns, and stormed inside. Carson and his squad circled Captain Tracy.

"Sir, what do we do?" Carson asked. "None of this has been approved—there's no intel, nothing."

"We stay onboard with Farouk and his guys," Tracy responded. "Right up until they're gonna do something really bad, like kill someone," he paused. "Right up until—and not before—and then we step in and stop them."

"Okay," Carson responded. "Okay—but this isn't what we were trained for—"

"They just killed his little brother and took off with his body," Tracy responded. "He's about to abandon us, and he's our only chance. He's the only one who can get a force to stand up to Al Qaeda on their own." Carson and the Marines of the squad stared at Tracy. "You all want to come home with a win?" the captain asked. "This is how we do it. This is the new game plan. It isn't what they taught you at Twentynine Palms during our workup."

The cries of a child echoed out of the house. The IPs dragged two women outside, then a six-year-old boy followed, his face dripping with tears. "The leader isn't here. This is his son," Farouk said. "We're going to kidnap him and trade him for the body of my brother."

"No," Tracy said, walking up to Farouk. "No. We're going to let them all go. They may be related to the leader, but that doesn't make them responsible for your loss."

"I know where the number two is, he's also here, in Haditha," Farouk said. His men began storming down an alleyway, their bats in hand.

"Sir?" Carson said to Tracy.

I've been in charge of this AO for less than two hours! Tracy thought.

"Sir? Do we follow them? Stop them? None of us have any idea of what is going on!"

"We're with the IP. We stand with them," Tracy said. "Let's go."

The Marines sprinted after the officers to a house surrounded by a concrete wall with a steel gate. WHACK! WHACK! One of the officers bashed the locked gate till it swung open. The IPs and the Marines stormed inside the compound's perimeter. *Our only intel is Farouk's word!* The words screamed in Tracy's head as he quickly pondered all that could go wrong—*probably a lot more than could go right at that moment.*

The IPs kicked open the front door of the house and lunged on a man in the entranceway, grabbing him by his hair and bashing his face against the wall.

"That's him," Farouk said. Farouk's officers swarmed through the house, searching for others, but they found only the one man, who Farouk claimed was the number two in AQI.

"Sir, we're going to search for any evidence," Corporal Carson said.

"Roger, Carson," Tracy responded.

Farouk screamed at the alleged AQI operative. He then backed off and spoke with one of his officers, who had come inside the house after a search of a rear courtyard. "We found the red Opel," Farouk said. "Do you know how many attacks this car has been involved in?"

The Marines combed the entire compound, searching for weapons, IED components, anything.

"He's a top commander," Farouk said. "He won't have anything like that here. He's too smart for that."

The Marines and the IPs brought the man back to their FOB and placed him in the small detention facility as they cross-referenced identifying information they found on him with intelligence databases to try to determine whether indeed he was a senior AQI operative.

"Sir, I need to let you know about a raid I just conducted," Matt Tracy said to Lieutenant Colonel Donnellan over a secure landline a few hours later, in the early morning of the twenty-fifth. Tracy described the events following the ceremony at the dam.

"No intel," Donnellan responded calmly. "No targeting data, no raid package, no approvals." Donnellan paused. The two discussed more details of the raid, the circumstances—including the AQI ambush and massacre that included Farouk's brother—and the importance of the police chief to the success of the battalion's mission of building an enduring security for the local population.

"We need him, sir," Tracy stated. "We need him."

"Yes, I know," Donnellan responded. "I'm well aware that we need him. So, you need to do what you need to do to keep him on the team, but remember, keep him in line." The two hung up just as a firefight erupted in the streets between an Echo squad and Al Qaeda operatives. AQI fired at the Marines with rocket-propelled grenades, machine guns, and AK-47s. The Marines took positions and fired back, and the attackers melted into the darkness.

A while later, in the early hours of daylight on September 25, Colonel Farouk approached the holding cell in which the purported AQI leader slept. "We need to speak with the prisoner," the police chief stated to the Marine guard. "We just need a few minutes with him."

"No," the guard responded. Once inside the wire of Echo Company's FOB, Tracy and the battalion "owned" the prisoner, meaning only they had authority over him.

"This is my country! This man is my prisoner!" Farouk yelled, then calmed a bit. "I need to ask him a few questions about my brother," he said. The young Marine guard knew the story of the police chief's younger brother's death just hours earlier.

After some thought, the guard acquiesced. "Okay," he said. "I'll just stand right here."

The Marine opened the cell, and Farouk and two of his men walked inside, waking the prisoner from sleep. Farouk and his men began speaking with the prisoner, calmly at first, then the back-and-forth soon became heated. Farouk and his officers screamed at the man. Sergeant Jason Matthews ran up to the cell when he heard the commotion.

"Get Captain Tracy!" the guard yelled to Matthews just as one of the officers punched the prisoner in the jaw. "Stop!" he yelled at Farouk.

"This is my country! My prisoner!"

Sprinting to get Matt Tracy, Matthews ran past Navy Hospital Corpsman Phillip "Doc Opie" Oppliger.

"Go check on the prisoner!" Matthews yelled. "They're beating him!" Matthews woke Captain Tracy from a brief nap, telling him of the events at the detention facility. Just as Tracy stood, Oppliger ran up.

"He's close to being dead," Doc Opie said. "The prisoner's barely alive. Farouk started working him over. He barely has a pulse." Tracy sprinted to the cell. The guard was trying to revive the man with CPR, which Oppliger had started. The prisoner's head flopped to the side after a few seconds.

"I'm getting this guy a medevac to Al Asad," Tracy said. "Where's Farouk?"

"He and his men already took off, sir," Doc Opie responded. Tracy sprinted to the COC and put in an urgent medevac call.

"Sir." Doc Opie bounded into the room minutes later. "Cancel the medevac." Tracy looked at Oppliger. "The prisoner's dead."

5

=== ★ ===

BROTHERS OF THE FIGHT

"THAT GUY WE DETAINED LAST NIGHT," TRACY SAID TO JIM Donnellan by phone, "the one we got with no raid package, and no targeting data—"

"Yeah," Donnellan responded.

"He's dead."

Donnellan said nothing for seconds. "Oh—" the battalion commander began. "Oh—kay," he said, followed by more silence. "I'll call you later."

"I'm done," Captain Tracy said to Darryl Atkins, Echo Company's first sergeant. "My bags aren't even unpacked, and I'm going to prison."

"That guy was bad, sir," Atkins responded.

"I know," Tracy said. "We don't know just how bad, though, and it doesn't even really matter. He was under our control. He was our prisoner. We are supposed to be acting as custodians of prisoners during their time here before they can get processed out. We're not supposed to be executioners, or enablers of executioners."

"He was under the IP's control, sir," Atkins responded. "It was one hundred percent on them."

"If Farouk accepts responsibility for the act," Tracy said.

As they talked, AQI attacks continued nonstop in all parts of 2/3's AO. Throughout the day, the enemy took aim multiple times at Whiskey, Golf, Fox, and Echo Companies. The attacks never lasted more than a minute and always ended with the ter- rorists retreating into the backdrop of the region—the very area the Marines had come to protect. They ducked behind dwell- ings, businesses, small crowds, and even individual people. For the Marines, the fight to maintain restraint and focus on the overall goal of the campaign proved as frustrating as the fre- quency of attacks by the assailants.

The operational tempo, or "op tempo," kept Captain Tracy busy through the day as he sent out multiple patrols. Farouk's killing of the prisoner, however, weighed heavily on the com- pany commander's mind. *Guyton will probably be in charge in a few hours once they arrest me,* he thought. He knew that Colonel Crowe had learned of the death and was in the process of opening a number of investigations. Later that night, Tracy returned to his room to get a few hours of sleep.

"Hello?" he said as he walked into his room. A Marine cap- tain stood there.

"I'm Billy Parker," the captain said. "I'm in charge of the Civil Affairs det[achment] here in Haditha." A member of the 4th Civil Affairs Group, a Marine Corps Reserve unit based out of Washington, DC, Parker ran what would become an in- tegral part of 2/3's efforts in Haditha to rebuild government and commerce, the Civil Affairs detachment. "When not acti- vated as a Marine, I work as a DEA agent, doing undercover work," he said. "And I have a law degree, and it sounds to me like you'll need a good lawyer," he said, smiling. "But why I'm here is to let you know that I think you're alright," he said. "I'd appreciate it if you stick around here, and not get hauled off to some prison."

"Appreciate your support, Billy, but I think things are set in motion at this point. It isn't up to me or you what happens. A guy died under my watch—beaten to death."

"A senior Al Qaeda operative," Parker responded. "Under the IP's watch."

"Have we confirmed that he was an AQI leader?" Tracy asked.

"No, not yet," Parker said. "But we'll find out his status soon enough."

The two viewed their roles in Haditha similarly and shared the same attitude and ideas about how to win the fight: act as a strong facilitator and supporter to allow the local police force to take over, and never back down and never waver during this rebuilding process. This introduction marked the beginning of a great working relationship built on trust and synergy.

"But not if they haul me off to prison," the Echo Company commander said. "And I can't even think about that now. The focus is on the fight. It's on the Marines. Winning. Right here, right now. Every minute, every second."

And every second of every minute would count.

THE FOLLOWING DAY, the twenty-sixth, would prove both brutal and critical for Echo Company. The brutality came first. Soon after dispatching the shot that killed Private First Class Christopher Riviere of Golf Company as he stood post in Haqlaniyah, the AQI sniper moved a few miles to the north, into the heart of Haditha. There, he waited, and watched, his weapon ready.

"I think I might have screwed up our route," nineteen-year-old Lance Corporal William Burke, of Echo Company, said.

"You're fine, Burke," Lance Corporal John "Mac" McClellan responded from about twenty feet behind Burke.

The two, part of an Echo Company foot patrol, had squeezed through the Mouse Hole ten minutes earlier. Now deep in the heart of Haditha, far outside the wire, Burke doubted himself.

As the designated "nav guy," his tasks included creating detailed routes and always knowing his squad's exact position, or grid. During this patrol, however, they found themselves closing in on an unfamiliar open space.

"You know where we're at," McClellan said reassuringly. "I know you do, Burke." McClellan, a veteran of 2/3's Afghan deployment, was a mentor to Burke, a newly minted Marine on his very first combat deployment.

McClellan, who had received two Purple Hearts during the Afghanistan deployment, had been with Burke during his first firefight a few weeks earlier. Pressed against a wall inside an abandoned house on the outskirts of Haditha at night, insurgent AK-47 rounds had whizzed in through a broken window inches from Burke. CRACK! CRACK! CRACK! Corporal Mario Anes and Sergeant William Davidson, also of Echo Company and also a veteran of 2/3's Afghan deployment, returned fire through that same window from inside the house. The yellow muzzle flashes from Anes's and Davidson's M16s brilliantly lit the inside of the room, and the CRACK! of each gunshot stung the Marines' eardrums. Seconds after the firefight started, the enemy "broke contact" and ran. The Marines in the room checked each other for injuries. Nothing.

As Burke emerged from the house after his first TIC, or "troops in contact," McClellan, who had been outside the house returning fire, sprinted up to him.

"Awesome, Burke! Awesome!" Mac had yelled at him, slapping Burke on his body armor. "All of us are always going to do everything we can do to get us through anything!"

On the foot patrol, Burke found himself sweating and breathing heavily. Having McClellan, Anes, and Davidson there didn't simply calm him but built a strength and composure through a brotherhood forged in combat. Each patrol with guys like McClellan boosted confidence, brought insight, honed his tactics and combat skills, and refined his focus on the mission. He'd rely on all of those components on patrol on the twenty-sixth.

"Get more dispersed," Anes yelled as they neared the large opening in the city. The Marines always patrolled "dispersed," or apart from one another, so as never to give an attacker a target larger than a single Marine. In wide-open areas, like the one they were preparing to cross, the rule was always to stretch that space between one another even farther.

Looking left, right, back at his map, then directly in front of him, Burke pressed onward—he was out front, "on point" on the patrol. Mac let Burke get a little farther ahead before he continued.

"Do the drunken monkey!" Anes yelled. "And do it quickly, let's push through this clearing fast!" The drunken monkey was a way of moving unpredictably: staggering steps, swaying back and forth, zig-zagging, bobbing one's head, so as not to give a sniper a predictable target.

Burke raced across the open space, flanked by Anes, then Mac followed, about thirty feet behind the two. Davidson approached from behind. All sprinted, aiming for a walled courtyard of what appeared to be an abandoned house.

POP! WHIZ! BANG! Anes heard the shot—and saw a yellow streak, like a tracer round or a spark of a bullet, hit a wall and ricochet. Anes and Burke dove for cover inside the courtyard, waiting for a second shot. It never came. "Marine down!" Anes yelled a second later. In the middle of the opening, a Marine lay facedown, motionless. The sniper had struck.

"Mac!" Burke yelled. "Mac!"

"We have to get him to safety," Anes said calmly as other Marines of the patrol stormed into the courtyard from other parts of the opening. "I think he's moving, just a little. We have to get him to safety." All inside, however, knew of a common enemy sniper tactic: shoot to wound, and then when others come to give aid, kill them, and then kill the first one shot.

The Marines couldn't fire even in the general vicinity of the sniper because they had no idea of his location—or if he was on the move at that point. They could have fired in all directions, then run out and carried Mac into the courtyard, but restraint—restraint—restraint when it came to pulling triggers in Haditha. Trigger fingers remained straight.

Anes and Burke looked at one another as Mac remained face-down on the ground. Then all at once, without anyone saying a word, Burke, Anes, and other Marines of the squad sprinted toward McClellan, forming a circle of protection around him.

This is a sniper's dream come true! An active sniper, and all of us are out here in the open, no cover anywhere around us! The words screamed in Burke's head as they rolled McClellan onto his back. *Who cares! I'd rather die trying to save John than live with myself afterward knowing that I didn't even try to save him!*

He'd been hit in the head. Blood poured from his face. His arms were limp. He didn't breathe. His face, colored purple, swelled. Unconscious, he teetered at the very precipice of death. Eduards "Doc" Primera, the Navy hospital corpsman attached to their squad, pulled off Mac's helmet and opened his airway.

"Burke! Give me our pos!" Sergeant Davidson yelled just after reporting a Marine down to the Echo FOB and requesting an urgent medevac.

"Let's get him back into the courtyard!" Anes roared. Anes and Burke lifted Mac, careful to keep his head steady, then sprinted toward the covered location as the other Marines maintained a "circle of life" around them, protecting them with their own bodies, each ready to take a round to protect Burke, Anes, and Mac.

"Pass me a grid, Burke! If you don't give me an accurate grid, this Marine's gonna die!" Davidson yelled. Burke carefully read off a ten-digit grid, indicating a position on the ground to a precision of one square meter. *I hope this is the right spot.* Burke recalled Mac's confidence in his navigation just minutes prior.

Davidson radioed the location to the Echo FOB. James Steuter and his squad, standing by as a QRF, or quick reaction force, raced to action as Captain Tracy requested an urgent Dustoff. The plan: Steuter's QRF would retrieve McClellan, then take him to the soccer field adjacent to the Echo FOB that served as an LZ, or landing zone. The Dustoff crew would put their Black Hawk down and then race him to Al Asad.

Please be right, Burke said to himself as Doc Primera fought to keep McClellan alive. The other Marines scanned the distance looking for any signs of another attack. *Please be the right grid! It's gotta be the right grid!*

As Steuter and his QRF raced down the streets of Haditha and the Army Dustoff crew rocketed through the air from Al Asad, two members of the Naval Criminal Investigative Service (NCIS) approached Captain Tracy in the Echo COC. "We've spoken to the Iraqi Police, and they haven't told us anything," one of them said. "They claim that they know nothing. We've got a dead Iraqi, and they aren't saying anything." Tracy still hadn't unpacked his bags. "Therefore, we have to read you your rights for murder."

"That's great," Tracy responded without pause. "But maybe you guys can wait around a bit to read me my rights. You see, one of my Marines, Lance Corporal John McClellan, who already has two Purple Hearts, just got shot in the head by a sniper and he's barely alive. I'd appreciate some space while I do my best on my end to see that he lives."

"There they are!" Sergeant Davidson yelled at the approaching convoy. "How's he doing?"

"He's still alive," Doc Primera said. "Barely."

The QRF came to a halt just feet from the Marines caring for McClellan—Burke's navigational prowess was right on the mark, as McClellan had known and had stated his confidence in just minutes earlier. The Marines loaded Mac onto one of the trucks. Doc Primera stayed by his side, continuing to do everything he could to see that he'd survive.

"He's gonna make it!" Steuter yelled. Doc Primera nodded at Steuter. "You're gonna make it, Mac! He's gonna make it! Let's go!" The convoy sped back toward the FOB—all the members knew that at any moment a huge explosion followed by a cloud of dark smoke, dirt, and dust could envelop them if they hit a massive IED.

But that didn't happen. They tore into the soccer field in just minutes, just as the Dustoff came inbound. Steuter and other Marines of the QRF helped the Army medevac personnel load Mac onto the "bird." It lifted into the sky and accelerated back to Al Asad.

They wondered if they'd ever see their friend again.

ANES CALLED IN to the Echo COC just after McClellan lifted off in the Dustoff Black Hawk. Captain Tracy answered. "Sir, we were wondering if we should end the patrol early due to what just happened."

"Negative!" Tracy responded. "You'll complete the patrol, then come back! Why would you want to come back early?"

"Roger that, sir," Anes responded.

Anes, Davidson, Burke, and others of the squad didn't run into any more enemy activity during the remainder of their patrol, although they tried. With the fate of Mac unknown, they just wanted to find the sniper, even if it meant drawing his fire.

They never found a clue. The streets remained empty, quiet, shadowed. The pallor of death hung low over them as they moved around the city. Near the end of the patrol, just before the call to RTB, or return to base, Captain Tracy passed great news to them: McClellan survived the flight to Al Asad. Doctors had stabilized him, and he was on his way to Landstuhl, a state-of-the-art American military hospital and trauma center in Germany.

"He's gonna make it," Tracy said.

"YOU LIKE HOW I do business?" Matt Tracy asked Farouk shortly after receiving word that McClellan was stabilized and en route to Landstuhl. "You like how we believed in you, worked with you, and helped you get that guy?" Farouk stared at Tracy, saying nothing. "You know, they are about to charge me with murder. They're going to take me away. You're never going to see me again. They're going to replace me with someone else." Tracy paused. "Who? How will the new guy work with you? Will he work with you at all? Or just make PowerPoints and wait for approvals from Al Asad?"

"We did nothing," Farouk said. "Nothing."

"Okay, then," Tracy responded. "Was nice knowing you." Tracy returned to the COC and continued to monitor the various radio nets as he awaited the return of the NCIS officers— waited for them to charge him with murder, and end not only his deployment but also his career.

"Captain Tracy."

Tracy turned to see the two investigators at the entranceway of the COC. One of them held a couple hats and some "challenge coins," small medallions commemorating individual military units.

"I've never spent much time around NCIS folks," Tracy responded. "I know every unit is different, with different customs, but do you NCIS people always bring hats and coins to people you are about to charge with murder?" The two investigators laughed.

"We spoke with Colonel Farouk and some of his officers," one of them said. "They said that it wasn't your fault. That it was their business, that the prisoner was under their custody," he paused, smiling. "Our work here is done. Investigation closed. Here, have these." They handed the hats and coins over to Tracy.

"Well, I guess I can unpack my bags," the company commander said.

"WE'RE BROTHERS," TRACY said to Farouk a few hours later. "We're in this together, to win, to set you and your IP force up to reclaim Haditha." Farouk remained stoic, unmoved. He struck Tracy as single-minded, focused, unyielding. The two spoke a bit more, then Tracy left.

"Number 2 AQI killed in Haditha, Iraq," the news ticker announced on a cable television station.

"That was the guy. The one Farouk killed with his bare hands. That was the guy," Tracy said shortly afterward to his Marines. "Just like Farouk said, number two AQI." Tracy paused. "Colonel Farouk killed him with his bare hands. He killed the guy who took part in beheading his IPs, including his little brother," he said. "For now on, we will stand in front of the IP. We'll take a bullet for them." The Marines before him nodded, smiling, understanding their commander's intent and outlook. "We are going to win, win this fight here in Haditha," he said. "These guys are brothers—we're all brothers—Brothers of the Fight."

JOHN McCLELLAN MADE it safely to Landstuhl, where surgeons further stabilized him. The military then flew him to the National Naval Medical Center in Bethesda, Maryland. The sniper's round had pierced McClellan's brain and left him with partial facial paralysis. That paralysis turned out to be temporary, however. Over the months, and then years, McClellan fully recovered. And though he didn't rejoin Burke, Davidson, Anes, Steuter, and others of Echo Company in Iraq, all kept him in their thoughts every day as they endured the toughest, most brutal fight of their lives.

6

= ★ =

THE EVERYDAY FIGHT

A TYPICAL DAY DOESN'T EXIST IN A WAR ZONE, ESPECIALLY IN AN AO like the Triad during 2/3's deployment there. After their first weeks on the ground, members of the battalion had experienced so much adversity, and witnessed so much violence and chaos, they soon grew accustomed to expecting virtually any event or eventuality. Nothing was typical, but nothing was surprising either. They took every day, every hour, every minute, every footstep one step at a time, always with winning the fight foremost in mind.

In addition to enemy action, the difficult and austere conditions of day-to-day existence pressed hard on the Marines of 2/3. They'd arrived in late summer in one of the hottest desert regions on the planet. During those first weeks, daily high temperatures averaged over 100 degrees Fahrenheit, with the heat often seeping long into the night. The battalion members needed to wear their PPE, or personal protective equipment, any time they ventured outside the interiors of their FOB's reinforced buildings. PPE includes a Kevlar helmet, ballistic goggles, and a flak jacket with ceramic SAPI (small arms protective insert) plates. Kevlar helmets act like convection ovens for the head, nearly cooking the brain. Just wearing one in the morning or evening brings streams of sweat. They're absolutely oppressive during midday movements and can cause heat stroke in the unprepared or uninitiated. Heavy flak jackets, which bite into shoulders and compress chest cavities, weigh upward of thirty pounds. Inflexible and cumbersome, the myriad straps and gear hanging from them catch on walls, concertina wire, seat belts, doorjambs, fencing, bushes—just about everything. Moving through any type of constricted environment, whether exiting a Humvee or shuttling through openings like the Mouse Hole, requires not only acuity but also extraordinary dexterity, and that comes only with practice. Just standing in place wearing a flak is exhausting; moving down streets, over walls, and up and down stairwells is almost superhuman.

Adding to the weight and cumbersomeness of their PPE were the gear racks, sidearms, backpacks, extra magazines, and grenades members of the battalion carried, plus the heavy boots and burly Marine Corps standard "digital cami" blouses and trousers they wore. Of course, each carried a service weapon, typically the M16, but sometimes the M4. Most service weapons included an accessory rail system and visualization aids like an advanced combat optical gunsight (ACOG) and an aiming laser/illuminator. Some had M203 40mm grenade launchers attached. With all the accessories attached, many service weapons weighed more than twelve pounds. Every member of the battalion kept his service weapon with him at all times, always.

None of the line company FOBs had running water except Echo Company's base in Haditha: it had a garden hose connected to a small rooftop water tank. For "hygiening" (shaving, brushing teeth, washing hands and face), most of the battalion used water from water bottles. For the occasional shower, they poked holes in water bottles. For relief, each FOB had "piss tubes" and "burn shitters." The tubes were PVC pipes buried at an angle in the ground. When a base had lye or gravel available, the Marines would make a leach field; otherwise, they'd just move the tubes when the odor became too strong. A burn shitter consisted of a plywood enclosure with a seat with a hole in it, under which sat a fifty-five-gallon drum cut down to a third of its height. Flies loved the burn shitters; Marines hated them. Marines hated the flies even more than the shitters because the insects swarmed inside the enclosure when someone entered—buzzing up through the hole in the seat. Everyone's greatest fear was dying on a burn shitter during a mortar or rocket attack. Even relieving oneself required full PPE at all times—"PPE to pee" some called it. "Shitter duty" ranked as the worst FOB chore. It was a daily necessity, typically assigned by schedule to a junior Marine (and sometimes bestowed as a punishment). The duty required the Marine to pull out the drum from under the seat, pour in JP-8 diesel-based jet fuel to make a soup-like consistency, light the mixture on fire, and stir till all burned off. This "flushing" turned the contents into black smoke and emptied the drum in about twenty minutes. The Marine burning and stirring made sure to keep away from the smoke.

Most of the battalion ate MREs (meals ready to eat) and "T-rats," or tray rations. Even the best "main courses" of MREs grew tiresome (chicken fajitas and barbecue burger were favorites), as did those of T-rats, which resembled camouflaged TV dinners but with far less flavor. Individually packaged muffins and beef jerky were some of the most welcome culinary treats at the FOBs, although they usually weren't available regularly.

Maintaining a consistent outside-the-wire presence meant that some Marines completed two, and sometimes three, three-hour patrols per day. Some patrols took them out for upward of a week. Between patrols coming and going into and out of the tight confines of the FOBs, and the mortar and other attacks, most Marines got only one or two hours of sleep at any given stretch. Furthermore, those cramped living quarters became large petri dishes when someone fell ill.

In short, the living conditions in the Haditha Triad were some of the bleakest, most austere anyone could imagine. After completing a patrol, a Marine often would then stand post, or do FOB chores (like flush a burn shitter), or maybe eat, or maybe sleep. Sometimes mail arrived. Sometimes there would be time to call home, but with time differences, that was often out of the question. Everyone lost weight. Everyone pondered their mortality. Everyone thought of those they'd left back home. Everyone looked to those around them—a family in the fight together.

But hardships and day-to-day rigors didn't slow the battalion down or ding morale in the slightest—even during those first weeks, which many considered "worse than hell," as Echo Machine Gunner Max Draper described it. The FOB would be their home for more than a half year. It didn't matter. It could be ten years. They'd make it.

The everyday fight the Marines waged during those first weeks intimately familiarized them with the lay of the land in each of their AOs. They learned the details of every street, every corner, each individual house—and they gained this knowledge not by following others, as during the left seat, right seat period, but by actually doing and leading the way themselves.

For Echo Company, this *doing* tightly incorporated Colonel Farouk and his IP into the company's patrols. Within a day of the NCIS investigators' departure (when Matt Tracy finally unpacked his bags), Marines of Echo conducted both daytime and nighttime patrols with Farouk and his men. These patrols, which often included Captain Tracy, arranged for individual squads to work with Farouk and the IP to gather intelligence during the day and then conduct raids at night. Within days, they uncovered IED cells, weapons caches, and yet more information on AQI operatives and suspected sympathizers.

During this period, Tracy, an ardent student of classic US Marine Corps warfighting technique, refined his own ad hoc version of counterinsurgency doctrine. Adding on to the outlook he articulated to his Marines after his one-on-one with Farouk, when he told them to be ready to take a bullet for the IP, he stated:

> You have to love the IP, you have to love the people of Haditha, you have to love them more than life itself. You have to genuinely be willing to lay down your life in this town—for the benefit of the IP, and ultimately, for the benefit of the people. The people here have to see this, to understand that you truly feel this, that *you* believe it and *live* it. We go to war fighting for the Marines next to us, so that we can be victorious and then all go home. But this is an insurgency, a political battle, and that has to do with trust. We have about a half year to go. We have to rid the city of AQI and get Farouk and the IP fully stood up so that the enemy will never return—and *we'll never have to return.* When we go out, when we get in a firefight, we're there for each other, but in this fight, we're there for each other to keep the mission going to completion, so that the IP can survive, and so in turn the people in this city can prosper and live their lives once again, to not have to be holed up in this ghost town living under the fist of Al Qaeda.

He told his Marines that this "doctrine" might require going beyond the normal call of duty: "Furthermore, you always have to be aggressive. Hyperaggressive. If there is an explosion, you run toward it. Run toward it without hesitation with the intent of stopping yet more violence. Run toward it to keep the people of the city safe. Put the well-being of the locals here above your own safety. Don't ever back down."

His message resonated with the Marines of Echo. While AQI continued to increase its attacks—across the entire Triad—the Marines in Haditha, learning more about the battlespace, the people, and the enemy each day—empowered by Tracy's ideas and leadership—formed a visceral understanding of how to keep constant pressure on the enemy.

WHAT ARE THOSE kids doing running away from that car? Corporal Aaron Rankin asked himself. An infantryman with Echo Company, he was manning an M2 .50 caliber machine gun in the turret atop a Humvee, the lead "vic," or vehicle, on a security convoy in Haditha that was accompanying an EOD (explosive ordnance disposal) team. The battalion had dispatched the EOD Marines to "reduce" (destroy by detonation) some enemy munitions discovered on the outskirts of the city. The job complete, Rankin's convoy was motoring along the final half mile to the base when he saw the children fleeing. "Something's about to happen," he mouthed, scanning in every direction. The Humvee's driver, Lance Corporal Zackeri "Zack" Drill, saw a black sedan up ahead. Rankin saw it, too. The car's white reverse lights lit and its tires screeched as it accelerated backward toward the Humvee.

"Stop!" Rankin yelled, reaching for the release on the turret so he could aim the .50 caliber machine gun. "STOP!" he yelled again to the car's driver. Then he noticed wires sticking out of the rear bumper of the car—a telltale sign of a pressure-plate trigger for an improvised explosive device. He immediately recognized that he and the others in the Humvee were possibly facing a suicide vehicle-borne improvised explosive device, or SVBIED. *Could be.* Or it could be a confused, innocent local. Fifty feet away, the car continued to accelerate in reverse. "STOP!" Then forty feet. It was coming fast. Thirty feet! "STOP!" The catch on the turret wouldn't release. He grabbed his M16 and flipped the fire selector from SAFE to SEMI as he raised the weapon. Then he aimed at the driver through the car's rear window. Twenty feet.

"Rankin!" Drill yelled. All in the Humvee knew that the car was likely loaded with hundreds of pounds of explosives. They'd all be killed within a fraction of a second. "RANKIN!!"

"STOP!!" Rankin yelled one last time and then squeezed the trigger. CRACK!—CRACK!—CRACK!—CRACK! The rear window exploded as ten rounds tore into the car. The driver slumped to the side. Drill screeched the Humvee to a halt.

BANG! The rear of the car smashed into the front bumper of the Humvee. No explosion. All let out a sigh of relief—it wasn't an SVBIED after all. Drill put the Humvee in reverse. He'd park on the side of the road so the Marines could see whether the driver had somehow survived the barrage of bullets Rankin had unleashed. Then both he and Rankin noticed the rear of the car—the Humvee's bumper had hit the car's trunk, above the exposed wires. *It might actually be an SVBIED, but we just didn't hit it on its pressure plate!* Drill thought, suddenly accelerating backward.

The car turned on its own and slowly drifted toward a shop on the side of the road. Its bumper hit the shop's concrete wall. Click! The impact pressed two spring-loaded slats of metal together, completing a detonation circuit. Electricity flowed into a line of artillery shells, each modified with a blasting cap. Tanks filled with "enhancing" propane surrounded the daisy-chained munitions packed in the trunk of the vehicle.

Rankin saw the car expand as if in slow motion, then lost consciousness a fraction of a second later as the blast wave enveloped him and the others in the Humvee. The massive explosion leveled the building and lifted the Humvee off the ground, slamming it down upright twenty feet away. The propane in the tanks created a massive fireball. The boom broke windows blocks away. A yellow and orange mushroom cloud, adorned with roiling black smoke, billowed hundreds of feet into the air. Three of the Humvee's four tires exploded. Flames engulfed the vehicle, setting it ablaze.

The expertly crafted SVBIED should have completely obliterated the vehicle—*should have*. The master AQI bombmaker had designed the weapon as a shaped charge, to blow almost all of its energy directly behind the car it was set in. And that's exactly what happened, but because the car had drifted and hit the shop on the side of the road, and not the Humvee, the explosion completely leveled the building. Still, because of their proximity to the blast, the kinetic, hyperbaric, and thermal energy easily could have killed all in the Humvee.

As the last of the fireball dissolved into the heights above, dust, dirt, rocks, and chunks of concrete rained down on the Humvee. The engine stopped. Radios fell silent. Nobody moved inside the flaming vehicle. BEEP! BEEP! BEEP! The "Chameleon," an electronic jamming device used to defeat IEDs triggered wirelessly, sounded its disabled signal.

PING! SNAP! SNAP! SNAP! PING! BOOM! PING! PING! BOOM! Just as the dust began to clear, Al Qaeda fighters, prepositioned in three areas for an ambush, opened up on the Humvee with rocket-propelled grenades, AK-47s, and a machine gun. Bullets "snapped" just above Rankin's limp body where he slumped on his back in the turret, ricocheting off the armor of the vehicle. The RPGs exploded on the shops adjacent to the blast site, just missing their mark. The clangs of bullets impacting the Humvee echoed throughout the smoking interior of the vehicle. BEEP! BEEP! BEEP! CLANG! CLANG!

"Huh?" Drill regained consciousness. "Rankin?" he mumbled. "Rankin!" he yelled. "Hunsberger!" Drill looked to his right to see Corporal John Hunsberger, his head cocked to the side. "Hunsberger!" Drill hit Hunsberger's helmet with the palm of his left hand.

"Drill?" Hunsberger mouthed. "Drill? What—where—"

"Rankin!" The pings of bullets and the beeps of the Chameleon continued. Drill looked up into the turret to see Rankin collapsed. Drill grabbed his M16 and rolled out of the Humvee. He checked his arms and legs. He was okay. Then he got down on one knee and started returning fire at all three AQI positions.

BOOM! An RPG exploded just feet from him.

"RANKIN!" Hunsberger lifted himself up from the passenger side of the Humvee and tried to check on Rankin as bullets slammed into the vehicle.

Then the enemy fire stopped.

Hunsberger jumped out and climbed up on the turret. Drill got back inside the burning Humvee to check the radios—all remained dead. He tried to turn over the engine. Nothing.

"Rankin!" Hunsberger yelled to Rankin as he grabbed him. He started praying to himself. "Rankin!" Rankin's M16 looked cartoonish—the barrel was twisted at a forty-five-degree angle. "Rankin!"

"My arm." Rankin regained consciousness. "I can't feel my right arm."

"You're alive! We're getting you back!" Hunsberger gasped. "Drill let's get out of here!"

"Won't start!"

"My arm," Rankin repeated. "I can't feel it."

Then the Humvee's diesel engine gurgled to life—just as another RPG came inbound. BOOM! More machine gun fire erupted. Drill floored the flaming Humvee and spun it around away from the gaping ten-foot-deep IED crater, racing away on one tire and three sparking rims.

The enemy broke contact as Marines in the other vehicles in the convoy put heavy machine gun rounds, medium machine gun rounds, and M16 rounds on top of all the AQI positions.

"We're almost there," Drill said, the Humvee filling with smoke. Seconds later, guards at the Echo FOB looked at one another as the Humvee, flaming, smoking, leaning to one side, and trailing a banner of sparks from the bare rims on the road surface, sped toward them. With no radios, Drill couldn't contact Echo base—but they passed inside the wire no problem because a Marine in another vehicle in the convoy, who had been trying unsuccessfully to raise Drill after the explosion, had realized their radios were out and called the Echo FOB for him.

Once it stopped, Marines at the FOB converged on the Humvee, fire extinguishers in hand, and put out the flames and got Rankin out of the turret. His arm had swelled to twice its normal size. They got him on the ground and pulled off his flak. BOOM! A 120mm mortar exploded in the soccer field. "Guess you're not gonna get flown out to Al Asad with them mortaring us!" Drill said. BOOM! Another mortar hit, closer than the first.

"He dislocated his shoulder," Hunsberger said.

"I don't know," Drill responded. "What do you have, X-ray vision?"

"Maybe the doctor should figure it out," Rankin said, still dazed from the massive car bomb. BOOM! Another mortar impacted, closer yet. "They're walking mortars onto our pos. They'll be inside the wire with the next one."

"Here, Drill," Hunsberger said. "Hold my M16 and watch this." He handed Drill his service rifle. "I'm going to reduce it and it'll be just fine." Hunsberger grabbed Rankin's right arm and twisted it.

"Wait!" Rankin yelled. "Uhhhhh!" He let out a roar of pain. BOOM! Another mortar impacted. "It's not dislocated! Something's broken! I can feel the bones grinding past one another!"

The Marines helped Rankin inside the safety of the main FOB building as the Humvee smoldered. A corpsman gave him painkillers and completed an initial examination.

Fifteen minutes later, Captain Tracy, standing over Aaron Rankin, said, "You saved a bunch of Marines, Corporal Rankin. That was some serious bravery there, Marine."

Rankin began fading in and out of consciousness. His stomach hurt. His arm continued to swell. His head pounded. Despite the painkillers, the agony took hold.

"You saved the day, Rankin," Tracy repeated. "And you lived. Good job." Rankin broke a smile. "You just earned yourself a ticket to Al Asad. Bird's inbound now that the Al Qaeda mortar guys have given us a break." Marines in the room loaded Rankin onto a stretcher to take him to the soccer field.

Bang! "Ugh!" The Marines carrying him accidentally jammed his right shoulder on a wall as they passed through a narrow doorway. Then, en route to the LZ in the back of a Humvee, he rolled off the stack of MRE boxes they had used as a makeshift bed for him. Finally—mercifully—Rankin was loaded onto the bird, and the Army Dustoff crew whisked him to Al Asad.

Another day in the Triad. He had saved lives with his actions, and saved his own because of the strict regimen of wearing PPE. He never would have survived that blast, which investigators later determined to be between eight and twelve artillery rounds strung together, enhanced by propane tanks, except for wearing all of his PPE.

Physicians determined that Rankin had suffered a traumatic brain injury (TBI) and a fractured right scapula. Doctors also discovered shrapnel in his face, but only after placing him inside an MRI machine, where his cheeks and lips seethed in pain when the strong magnetic field pulled on the bits of metal buried in his flesh. He eventually made it to Germany, and fully recovered from his injuries.

A few hours after the explosion, Drill, Hunsberger, and others of the section once again departed from the Echo FOB on another patrol of the city.

7

★

AO ON FIRE

DESPITE THE PROGRESS THE MARINES MADE IN SECURING THE Triad—notably with the assistance of Colonel Farouk and the IPs in Haditha—more of the most-hardened, experienced AQI fighters flowed into the AO day after day during the early part of 2/3's deployment. By the end of the second week, the entire region had erupted into a conflagration of violence and tumult. Mortar attacks continued unabated, as did well-planned and complex ambushes, rocket attacks, and the two most insidious dangers: IEDs and sniper attacks. The Island Warriors were not even into their third week of deployment when they would suffer their greatest single-day loss so far, on October 8.

"Okay, let's sweep," said Sergeant Andrew Niccum, a section leader in Fox Company. Niccum was in charge of his "section" of vehicles, itself a component of a MAP, or Mobile Assault Platoon. The convoy had come to a stop, and the Marines fanned out as ordered, looking, searching, scanning for any signs of hidden IEDs. Eyes down, scanning left, then back to their feet, then forward a bit, then right. They looked for signs of "command wire"—long stretches of thin wire used to trigger an IED remotely. They looked for stacks of rocks used by a remote trigger person, who would determine when to set off a blast. They looked for disturbed ground, possibly telling of a recently hidden "package" of explosives. They looked for discoloration of the pavement. They even looked for antennas near the road. Any telltale sign.

If someone found something, they'd call an EOD team to inspect the evidence. The inspection would often include the use of a robot called a "MARCbot" to keep personnel at a safe distance. If an IED was found, the EOD team would reduce the device with an explosion, allowing the convoy to continue on its way.

Niccum's convoy had just visited the Haditha Dam. The safest part of the AO, with good "standoff" from any potential enemy attack and built of steel-reinforced concrete, the dam was the only place where members of the battalion weren't required to wear PPE at all times. The dam also had functional plumbing, warm water, showers, laundry facilities, an MWR (morale, welfare, and recreation facility—a room with computers with internet access and phones to call home), and a chow hall. Convoys from all companies made regular trips to the dam to get supplies, repair equipment, and retrieve mail. But the route to and from the dam proved to be one of the most dangerous in the entire AO because AQI knew that convoys frequently plied that passage through the desert.

Convoys always stopped at any sign of a possible IED. They also always stopped at "Tier 1" sites—places that, whether a Marine eyed a sign of a potential IED or not, had proven to be the highest-probability areas for the weapons to be employed. One such spot was a bridge over a wadi, or dry ravine, roughly halfway between Barwana and the dam.

Over the years, AQI had become very creative with how it emplaced explosives in and under bridges and other forms of infrastructure. The terrorist group laid some of its most deadly IEDs by burrowing into a roadway from under a bridge span.

One operative or a group of them would first dig into the road. Then another would place explosives, followed by someone affixing the trigger mechanism. The triggers were either victim-actuated ones, like a pressure plate or a tripwire, or remote, detonated by a hidden trigger man who would send a signal over a hard wire or wirelessly with a cellular phone or two-way radio. Through experience, AQI had marshaled its skill at crafting deadly IEDs, hiding them, triggering them, and then slipping away into the desert in the wake of the destruction. Although the Marines found many IEDs over their first weeks in the Triad, some devices went undetected.

"Jones, go ahead and get in that seven-ton," Niccum said to Corporal Derek Jones, of Fox Company, at the end of the sweep. Riding high off the ground on its large wheels, and built of thick, heavy steel, seven-tons could take much more IED punishment than lower-riding, lighter vehicles like Humvees. That steel, however, very effectively transmitted energy from an explosion.

Jones climbed up the steel "stairs" on the rear of the lead seven-ton of the convoy and sat in the back on one of the benches that lined each side of the truck. As Niccum and others finished up the sweep in the sweltering heat of the day, he readied to "mount back up" and continue toward Barwana.

CRACK! Niccum felt the concussive blast a fraction of a second before the explosion smacked his ears. He locked his eyes toward the seven-ton into which Jones had just climbed. He saw only a cloud of rising brown dust.

"Jones!" Niccum sprinted toward the seven-ton. "Jones!"

"Jones is in bad shape, sergeant," a Fox Company Marine said to him as he reached the truck. Niccum climbed into the truck, then slowly descended to the ground.

"No, he didn't make it," Niccum said. "Search for other IEDs and let's find the trigger man if there is one!" Anger coursed through Niccum's veins. He thought of the times he'd spent with Derek Jones, a friend. Niccum had been a mentor to the twenty-one-year-old. *He got to speak with his wife yesterday,* he thought. *I'm so thankful for that.* Niccum burned to find the people responsible for the act. He thought of the November 19, 2005, killings in Haditha and the IED strike that preceded the actions of the 3/1 Marines. *I can see how a war fighter can become a killer. I can understand it. I want retribution.*

He scanned all around him, looking in the distance for movement and closer to the site of the explosion to see if there were any signs of command wire blown into view by the blast—command wire that he and other Marines could follow to the site of the trigger man. *Nothing. Ghosts. Phantoms.*

The Marines of the convoy swept and swept and swept in the cruel heat in the aftermath of the terrible loss. No more signs of IEDs, and no sign of anyone responsible for the death of Derek Jones. They mounted up and continued to the FOB at Barwana.

AROUND THE SAME time, an Echo Company patrol pushed into the heart of Haditha. CRACK! As they crossed a street adjacent to a palm grove, the sound of a single gunshot echoed throughout the area. A Marine fell to the ground.

The others in the patrol spun around looking east only to see a large black sedan, roughly a hundred meters distant, slowly leaving the area. Two Marines raised their weapons. Through their sights, they each saw that the car was missing its left taillight assembly. Based on the geometry of the situation, the shot couldn't have originated from anywhere other than that car. Both Marines flipped their fire selectors from SAFE to SEMI on their M16s. Each began squeezing their trigger with their gun sights trained on the head of the driver. *Wait!* A group of innocent locals walked between the Marines and the sedan. They straightened their trigger fingers. The vehicle disappeared around a bend.

The two Marines ran to their comrade on the ground. Others were kneeling next to him. He stood up on his own, smiling—the round had ricocheted off his Kevlar helmet, leaving just a laceration. They reported the incident and an immediate BOLO, or "be on the lookout," call went out over Echo Company's net. The attack mirrored others in the area in the past week—a single shot, to the head or torso, like the one that hit Mac, like the one that killed PFC Riviere, and like the one that hit and deflected off of a Golf Company Marine's helmet just prior to PFC Riviere's death.

"It's our sniper," Matt Tracy said in the Echo's COC (combat operations center). "But he's not a sniper—he's not using a sniper rifle, anyway. He shot from a hundred meters away, and the bullet didn't penetrate a Kevlar helmet? What kind of weapon is this guy shooting with?" he paused. "And why did Anes report seeing a streak, like a tracer round? Snipers never shoot with tracer rounds."

Shortly after the BOLO call went out, an Echo Company mounted patrol roared through an intersection in another part of Haditha. "It's the black sedan!" Lance Corporal Jeremy Sandvick Monroe said from the vehicle commander's seat of one of the convoy's Humvees. They circled around an adjacent city block and then halted, with Sandvick Monroe's vic stopped in the middle of the intersection. Lance Corporal Jared Campbell, another Echo Marine, rode in the Humvee directly behind Sandvick Monroe. He watched as Sandvick Monroe exited the vehicle, then sprinted toward its rear, looking in every direction for the black sedan—always moving, never giving a potential enemy a static target. Then, just as Mario Anes had seen days before during the patrol with John McClellan, Campbell saw a glimmer of light streak past him and shoot straight toward Sandvick Monroe. In a tiny slice of a second, the flash seemed to circle around Sandvick Monroe's head, then disappear just below his helmet. He dropped straight to the ground.

"Jeremy!" Campbell bounded out of the Humvee and raised his M16 rifle, scanning the distance in the direction of the streak. "Nothing," he mouthed to himself. "Just the city."

And then, just out of sight, a black sedan, missing its left taillight assembly, slipped around a corner into the maze of Haditha. Gone again.

The Marines of the squad fought to save Sandvick Monroe's life. They pulled off his helmet, opened his airway, and pulled gear off of him. Sandvick Monroe, a veteran of 2/3's Afghan deployment, was well known throughout Echo Company and universally liked and admired. A SAW (squad automatic weapon) gunner when he was in Afghanistan, Sandvick Monroe often took the point position on patrols through the rugged and unforgiving Hindu Kush. Tall and lanky, he never seemed to tire, and always smiled, even in tumult and adversity.

A corpsman and two others carefully lifted him into the rear of a seven-ton as Marines kept a protective circle around them. Each one scanned, looking for another potential attacker. With Sandvick Monroe secure, the convoy raced back to the Echo FOB as a Dustoff lifted off from Al Asad. By the time Sandvick Monroe was inside the wire of the base, he'd taken his last breath. He was twenty-one years old.

"Tell me it's not him," shouted Mario Anes, who had deployed to Afghanistan in Echo Company with Sandvick Monroe the year before. Both served as SAW gunners. "Tell me it's not true!" Anes roared, running up to Lance Corporal Matthew Darland, one of Jeremy's closest friends. Darland just stared at Anes blankly, his eyes swollen. "No!" Anes threw his arms around Darland, who stood stone-faced and motionless. "Man, no!" Tears pooled in Anes's eyes. "NO!"

8

=== ★ ===

FLY LIKE A WINGED
BAT MONKEY FROM HELL

WHO'S NEXT? ANES PONDERED THE LOSS OF SANDVICK MONROE as he sat on his rack in his room after letting go of Darland. *Who will die next?* "I'm twenty years old," he said out loud to himself, then closed his eyes and buried his face in his hands. *I'm not ready to go. I can't go. I can't believe Jeremy's gone. I can't believe he's gone. I can't believe it.*

Shut up and be strong.

BOOM!

The sound crashed through the depths of the night, echoing across the Triad. Captain Tracy stared at the radios in front of him, waiting for them to begin blaring, signaling that a Humvee or a seven-ton had hit an IED. Seconds passed. Then a minute passed. Then two minutes. The radios remained silent. Then some calls came through. Various units wondered whether the blast had hit any Marines. An Echo squad pushed out and found a government building leveled, but no dead or injured people. Just the building, destroyed. The Marines would later learn that

AQI had bombed the building because of its importance to locals: they met there to discuss a democratic way forward for their government. They also used it as a makeshift disco.

"The radios didn't light up immediately because it didn't involve any of us!" Captain Tracy roared. A few of his Marines were with him. They had traveled to the dam and would return to Haditha the next morning. Farouk had recently discussed with Tracy how the townspeople felt about the Americans, and Tracy relayed this to his Marines that night.

"We have to win their respect! You can't just jump into action when it is one of us. You have to put them first, as I've been saying. You have to prove yourselves to the people of Haditha—when you hear an explosion, you can't just wait around and head out when it's another Marine," he said. "You have to orient yourself toward the inferno, and fly like a winged bat monkey from Hell!"

Mike Scholl, James Steuter, and a couple of the other Marines started laughing.

"It's not funny! I mean it! We have to win the respect of the people here by proving to them that we mean what we say!" He paused. "You have to love this town! Love the people of the town. It isn't about us, it isn't about me, it's about them! They are the special people!" He paused again. "Rush into the fire to save them even before we'll rush into the fire to save one of us! You hear an explosion, or there is a firefight, fly like a winged bat monkey from Hell! Concerns about battlefield geometry be damned! Concerns about friendly fire be damned! Just trust your gut and go!"

Earlier that day, just after an AQI improvised explosive device killed Derek Jones and a sniper took the life of Jeremy Sandvick Monroe, a squad of Marines had slipped through the Mouse Hole into Haditha. Although the patrol began from the Echo FOB, only half of the group hailed from Echo Company. The other half belonged to Headquarters & Services, specifically, a platoon from H&S: Scout Snipers. The team blended in with the patrol—everyone carried the same type of weapon, had the same type of side arm, and, of course, wore the same "Marpat" (Marine pattern) digital camis and the same boots. The scout snipers weren't out with the Echo Marines to set up an ambush on AQI but were on a reconnaissance mission. The team, led by Corporal Joe Roy, who had been integral in a number of pivotal battles during 2/3's Afghan deployment, would identify a "hide house" where they would return later in the night.

Scout snipers perform critical functions for Marine Corps infantry battalions, and members of these little-known and less understood teams proved invaluable to 2/3 from the moment they arrived in the Triad. Far more than just blending into the background of a battlespace and taking shots against enemy targets hundreds of meters distant, Marine scout sniper teams perform a spectrum of roles: They act as the battalion's "eyes forward," providing a broad overview of the battlespace and detailed views of individual corners of a region, or of specific enemy personnel. They undertake surveillance and reconnaissance missions for future patrols and large operations. They provide "overwatch" of larger units of Marines, identifying potential ambushes and then interdicting those preparing to launch such attacks with "well-placed rounds" from concealed hides. They also plan and execute missions like the one Roy and his team began when they slipped through the Mouse Hole with the Echo Marines: interdiction of enemy personnel.

Most of a scout sniper's time spent on the ground involves observation, not shooting. They observe individual people, groups, buildings, routes, and key terrain features. They look for patterns and cycles and try to identify anomalies in a scene—such as individuals acting in a way that might indicate an enemy ambush about to explode onto a patrol.

During the patrol that day, Roy and the other scout snipers, in addition to aiding the Echo Marines with their duties, observed buildings and urban geometry in the north side of

Haditha, notably, near the palm groves. They were looking for a place to "set up shop" for the upcoming "period of darkness"—the dark hours after sunset until the next morning.

Just as the Euphrates River corridor served as a conduit for Al Qaeda to strategically move in, out, and through Iraq during the course of the war, the palm groves served a tactical purpose for enemy fighters, who concealed themselves in the trees during their movements and allowed the trees to provide cover during firefights. AQI operatives could take a boat to an "insert point," travel up and down the river under the hide of the groves, strike, and then egress to an extract point on the river. The groves were dense enough to provide cover but open enough to allow easy and fast passage. The Marines of 2/3, of all companies, quickly learned that not only did the enemy use the palm groves to their advantage but also the trees played integral roles in most enemy operations.

By the end of the patrol with the Echo Marines, Roy and his Scout Sniper team had identified a house that would provide the overwatch they sought. Hours later—just before the explosion that leveled the meeting/disco government building—Roy and his team once again slipped through the Mouse Hole. Soon, they entered a courtyard and tapped on the door. A family let them in, and Roy and his Marines first apologized profusely, then explained, in broken Arabic, that they'd need to use a specific upstairs bedroom for twenty-four hours. They also told the family that everyone would need to remain in the house for that entire span of time and not answer the door or make any phone calls. The family agreed, and even brought tea. Roy and the other scout snipers set up shop, then waited for dawn to crack open a new day in the town.

"Request permission to engage," Captain Tracy heard over one of the Echo Company nets as he and the others who had visited the dam for the night sped back toward Haditha. Joe Roy and his scout snipers had positively identified AQI fighters loading weapons into a vehicle across the street from their hide. Roy was addressing Nic Guyton, Echo's executive officer.

BOOM! A massive explosion rocked the northern portion of the city as Roy and Guyton went back and forth for the approval process. The explosion was just a few blocks from the scout snipers' hide.

"Go!" Captain Tracy yelled to his driver. "Fly like a winged bat monkey from Hell to that explosion!" The drivers of all the convoy's vics floored their accelerators. "Fly like a winged bat monkey from Hell!"

The radio nets exploded. "They're getting into the car to head over to the blast that just happened," Roy said to Lieutenant Guyton. "I need approval right now or they're gone and will ambush the QRF!"

An SVBIED had smashed into a Marine Corps M1A1 tank and detonated. The massive explosion knocked one of the tracks off the Abrams and knocked the four tankers inside unconscious. Flames engulfed the wreckage of the car and the tank. An Echo quick reaction force sped out of the FOB to provide aid—and the AQI fighters in the crosshairs of Joe Roy's team readied to meet them.

"Take them," Guyton said. "You're approved." Guyton then immediately ordered another QRF to depart to extract the Scout Sniper team; although they'd take out the AQI operatives, they'd also compromise their location. They needed to kill the enemy fighters, then get out as quickly as possible.

Roy "unsafed" his M40A3 bolt action sniper rifle and gently squeezed the trigger, in perfect timing with the beat of his heart and his breathing. The driver's head exploded. Roy chambered another round. Three gunmen jumped out of the car with their AK-47s and searched frantically for the location of the shooter—the hunters now the hunted. Roy calmly squeezed the trigger of the A3 again. One of the fighters dropped to the ground; a pool of blood grew outward from his head. The other two took cover and tried to aim a shot at the window through which Roy's two deadly bullets had passed.

As Captain Tracy's convoy and the first Echo QRF screamed toward the site of the disabled tank, other AQI fighters took position, waiting for the Marines to come to the aid of the Abrams crew.

CRACK! A third trigger squeeze, and a third kill for the Scout Sniper team. One to go. The last fighter jumped out into the street and started spraying bullets at the house from which the team killed with such precision. CRACK! That Al Qaeda member dropped to the ground.

"Let's go," Roy said. "Let's pack up and wait for the QRF and get out of here." He paused, smiling. "Hopefully some of their friends will come to get them and we can take them, too."

"Look!" Matt Tracy's driver yelled, slamming on the brakes. Four sedans sped in front of the convoy from a side street. Tires screeched as the sedans spun out.

"These guys are bad!" Tracy yelled. "Dismount!" The company commander, in the lead vic, swung open his door. The sedans crashed to a halt less than ten feet from the nose of Tracy's Humvee. Ten men emerged, all armed with AK-47s. Tracy raised his M4 as the men raised their weapons. He flipped his fire selection switch from SAFE to SEMI just as the windshield of the lead sedan exploded. A metallic CLANK!—CLANK!—CLANK!—CLANK! pierced the air as the machine gunner in Tracy's Humvee opened up with "the fifty" only a few feet to the side of the captain. The men before him started to scatter, ducking down and raising their weapons and firing. CRACK! CRACK! CRACK!—CRACK! Tracy dumped rounds into the AQI assailants, then Mike Scholl, on the rear seven-ton, took aim with his .50 caliber machine gun. Al Qaeda heads split open, tires burst, windows shattered, blood flowed down the street.

"Run like a cheetah, Steuter!" Tracy yelled, ejecting a spent magazine. Steuter took his place while Tracy slapped in his second mag. Steuter then jumped up on the lead sedan, searching for any AQI hiding behind the other cars. CRACK! CRACK! CRACK! "Like a cheetah, Steuter!" Tracy yelled, then fired off more rounds from his M4. One of the terrorists jumped to his feet from behind the farthest sedan and charged toward the Marines, firing his AK. Steuter flew off the roof of the sedan, firing at the assailant while in midair. "Like a CHEETAH!" Tracy yelled as the man's jaw flew off in the hail of Steuter's shots. "Awesomeness reigns, Steuter!" CRACK! CRACK!—CRACK!—CRACK!—CRACK! He'd hit him no less than seven times.

"Guess what, Marines?" Tracy yelled. He, Steuter, and three other Marines quickly inspected the enemy vehicles and the bodies.

"What, sir?" Corporal Steuter responded calmly.

"We just ambushed the ambushers. They were expecting us to get to the site of the explosion and ambush us there. We ambushed the ambushers!"

The pungent stench of burning flesh filled the air. Streams of blood, radiator fluid, and gasoline ran down the street amid hundreds of spent shell casings. The Marines safed their weapons and jogged back to their vehicles.

"Okay, Marines!" Tracy yelled. "Let's keep flying like winged bat monkeys from HELL!" Steuter and others laughed, then the four-truck convoy continued to the site of the explosion, just a few blocks distant.

None of the Marines had seen or even heard of a suicide vehicle-borne IED attacking a tank before. They turned a corner and rolled up to the scene: the tank with wreckage of a car plastered to its side. The convoy came to a halt, and Tracy jumped out and climbed through the flames to the top of the tank turret, then opened it. "I can't see," the tanker said. The QRF Guyton had dispatched arrived then.

"You're okay," Tracy said, "but, wow, that was a big explosion."

"Yeah, you're telling me," the tanker said.

"Let's get these guys medevac-ed and arrange for the tank to get pulled out of here," Tracy ordered.

The tankers had received minor wounds, but all would recover fully. None of the Marines of Tracy's convoy got even a scratch. Tracy and his convoy returned to a hero's welcome at the FOB. All the Echo Marines lined up—they'd been listening to the events unfold as they happened—and cheered them as they walked up to the COC. Tracy used the opportunity to give another of his motivational speeches about their fight and the outlook he wanted them all to have for the people of Haditha, punctuating it with his trademark "fly like winged bat monkeys from HELL!"

9

══ ★ ══

"DRILL"ING SNIPERS
WITH A SHOTGUN

DESPITE THE DAY'S SUCCESSES, THE DEATHS AND INJURIES IN-flicted by AQI weighed heavily on the members of the battalion, and in particular, those of Echo Company. While mission fidelity and friendships among Echo Company Marines grew stronger, many privately began to wonder whether they'd ever see home again, especially after McClellan's near fatal injury and the loss of Jeremy Sandvick Monroe. To many, the best therapy was simply being outside the wire—patrolling, patrolling, and then more patrolling. The days and nights proved exhausting, but the constant danger kept every Marine's acuity razor sharp.

The Echo Company Marines also had a "warrior-philosopher" in Captain Matt Tracy, whose tenacity, drive, vision, and from-the-front leadership style buoyed their spirits and cemented their resolve. Thoughts of Tracy bellowing "Like a CHEETAH!" and "fly like winged bat monkeys from HELL!" during combat brought smiles and laughter to Marines like James Steuter and

Mike Scholl. They laughed not out of mockery for their commander but out of reverence for his sheer audacity and unorthodox ways of keeping a mission flowing forward. *Who wouldn't follow a guy like that into the worst place in the world? He literally jumped through fire to open up a tank and then started yelling to go after a guy like a CHEETAH!*

Tracy not only would do (and did) what he told those under him to do but also did more than he'd ever ask any of his Marines to even attempt. And because of that, they all took every word of his to heart, and they admired and respected him more every day.

CRACK!—CRACK!—CRACK! A three-round burst exploded on a wall just above the head of Echo Marine Corporal Derek Lowe during a patrol in Haditha. Lowe and other Marines of his squad took cover and scanned the surroundings for the origin of the fire. Just over one hundred meters distant, a black sedan, with its left taillight assembly missing, crept away around a corner. Lowe immediately called it in. A mounted patrol that included Corporal John Hunsberger and Lance Corporal Zack Drill sped toward the location to begin the hunt.

"Hey, look," Drill said to Hunsberger just minutes later. "There it is, the black sedan with the missing left taillights!" Drill, the driver of the lead Humvee of the mobile patrol, accelerated toward the car. The sedan sped away.

"That's him," Hunsberger said. "That's got to be him, for sure." Drill flashed his lights, and the turret gunner, Lance Corporal Erick Gutierrez, yelled for the car to stop. It kept accelerating. "Shoot him!" Hunsberger yelled.

BRRRRRRRRRRRR! Gutierrez opened up on the sedan with a volley of 7.62mm rounds from his M240 machine gun. The driver slumped onto the steering wheel and the car slammed into a wall with a CRUNCH!

"Look!" Drill yelled, pointing. Three men leapt from the sedan. One held an AK-47, one carried a Dragunov sniper rifle, and one wielded an M16 fitted with a suppressor, an ACOG (advanced combat optical gunsight), and a portion of an M203 40mm grenade launcher.

POP!—POP!—POP! The fighter with the AK-47 took cover and began firing at the Marines. The one with the Dragunov bolted out of sight. CLICK!

"Jammed!" Gutierrez yelled. His M240's belt-fed ammunition had bound up in the gun's feed tray. Enemy rounds snapped and whizzed overhead.

The man with the Dragunov had taken up a position to fire on the Marines. The M16-wielding man ran down the street, searching for a covered position from which to engage the Humvee.

In a blur of motion, Gutierrez slammed the gun's charging handle to the rear. *KER-CHUNK!* Then he popped open its feed tray cover, swept and shook the rounds, slapped the cover closed, and then "sent the bolt home" by releasing the charging handle.

"Shoot them, Gutierrez!" Hunsberger yelled. "Shoot all of them! Zip 'em up! SHOOT THEM!" Gutierrez aimed and squeezed the trigger. Nothing.

"SHOOT THEM!" repeated Hunsberger, now outside the Humvee and taking aim. Gutierrez grabbed his M16 and aimed at the fighter shooting with the AK-47.

CRACK! CRACK! Gutierrez hit him once in the shoulder and once in his torso. He fell to the ground, then rolled over. Then a torrent of rounds burst from the AK-47. *He flipped it to full auto,* Gutierrez thought, as errant rounds buzzed over the top of the Humvee. *He's desperate.*

The bleeding fighter released the trigger and then took careful aim, directly at Gutierrez's head, but it was too late. The turret gunner—without a working turret gun—squeezed the trigger of his M16 just a fraction of a second before the enemy fighter could squeeze his. CRACK! The man fell back onto the pavement next to the crashed car. The fighter with the M16 bolted.

"I'll get him!" Drill grabbed a 12-gauge pump action shotgun and jumped onto the street. Loaded with slugs, the weapon was meant for breaching locked doors and gates, not for a fire-fight. Drill lunged after the AQI fighter as two of the man's compatriots flopped around in pools of their own blood.

"Wait!" Hunsberger roared. "Drill! Wait! I'm right behind you! You can't be running around alone!"

"Those two guys are wounded!" Drill yelled as he sprinted away. "You guys take care of their weapons! I'm going after this guy!" Ten steps later, the fighter turned into an alleyway and dropped his M16. Drill glanced at the gun on the ground as he raced by it. *Part of a 203?* he thought. *And a suppressor?* But the M16 wasn't loaded. Its magazine well was empty. Useless to the terrorist.

POP! POP! POP! The fighter shot back at Drill with a 9mm pistol. Drill crouched low and then unsafed the shotgun. He stood and took aim. BOOM! Click-Click. BOOM! Click-Click. Drill unleashed two rounds. They missed. He needed to get much closer to hit the guy with slugs. The Marine bounded down the alleyway and closed the gap, disappearing from the sight of Hunsberger and Gutierrez.

The fighter raced toward the end of the alleyway, capped by a chain-link fence. He lunged upward, desperate to escape. Halfway to the top, he shot at Drill again. POP! POP! He clawed his way higher as Drill lined up his shot. POP!—POP!—POP! The rounds snapped past Drill.

BOOM! Click-Click. BOOM! Click-Click. BOOM! Click-Click. Drill unleashed five rounds just as the fighter grasped for the top of the fence. He didn't make it. Chunks of his torso blew into the air as gravity pulled him down, back first. He was dead before he even hit the road.

"Drill!" Hunsberger yelled, rounding the corner into the alley-way. Drill strolled up to him with his shotgun over his shoulder.

"Got him," he said. "Now let's check out his weapon."

An up-close inspection revealed that what looked like an M16 was in fact an M16. After detaining the two injured fighters and taking their weapons, the Marines returned to the Echo FOB. The Iraqi Police towed the sedan for the Marines to inspect. The two wounded AQI members were flown to the aid station at Al Asad and would then be sent to a detention facility. Hours later, Captain Tracy assembled Drill, Hunsberger, and others of the company not outside the wire.

"Well, this is most of our sniper team," Tracy said. "Or *was*—thanks to Drill and his shotgun and Gutierrez and his M16. They removed the left taillight and found a hide built in the trunk of the car," Tracy said. "And so the driver would move around Haditha and Haqlaniyah, and they'd just wait till a patrol passed by, and then strike."

"Where'd he get that M16?" Drill asked. "It looks like one of ours, but it has a suppressor."

"It is one of ours," Tracy responded. "Well, not one of 2/3's, but it belongs to the Marine Corps." He paused. "You all are familiar with 3/25, right? The battalion that took it so hard here a little more than a year ago?" All in the room nodded. "I just called in the serial number on this weapon. It belonged to Sergeant Rock, one of 3/25's snipers that AQI overran and killed right here in Haditha. This AQI sniper team's been hitting us with our own weapon."

"And using our ammo," Drill said.

"Right, Drill," Tracy said. "Hence the tracer rounds that have been reported during strikes. Great job. Three fewer bad guys, and we got the Marine Corps its M16 back." Captain Tracy smiled at Drill. "Maybe next time wait for Hunsberger to join you. It's a dangerous city to be running around by yourself in. And don't forget—we still have this guy with the Dragunov out there. And who knows if there are other cars with hides in the trunk. I'd be willing to bet that they do."

News of Echo Company's successes spread throughout the entire battalion within hours. Although the enemy had been quickly evolving its tactics to gain a foothold in the city of

Haditha, Tracy had focused on the fundamental characteristic to keep his Marines one step ahead of the enemy: hyper-aggressiveness. With that posture, and with unmitigated support for the people of the city and the Iraqi Police, the captain believed that he and Echo Company were one great step closer to victory in their AO.

A half year remained, however, and they'd already suffered immense losses. Much would happen in that time, good and bad.

10

WHISKEY'S OPENING FIGHT

While members of H&S, Echo, Fox, and Golf Companies were first stepping onto their AO after having flown from Al Asad to the Haditha Dam, members of 2/3's reorganized Weapons Company, Whiskey, set off from the large base on a ground convoy to the town of Baghdadi. Baghdadi, which lies along the Euphrates River corridor adjacent to Al Asad about twenty miles south of the core of the Triad, would be home to Whiskey for the first two months of its deployment. Then the company would move north to Albu Hyatt, just south of Haqlaniyah.

During the 1970s, the Saddam Hussein regime had built an extensive resort complex in Baghdadi for Saddam's Ba'ath Party officials and their families. He also constructed a sizable military complex adjacent to the resort area. The town, which lies on the edge of a large oxbow meander of the Euphrates, is set against a starkly beautiful backdrop. Fringed by verdant palm groves, the azure waters of the Euphrates contrast with both the surrounding sun-beaten desert and the muted sky. Baghdadi served well as an "oasis" for the center of power in Baghdad, just over one hundred miles distant.

A weapons company in a Marine infantry battalion is typically composed of seasoned, highly experienced personnel, both enlisted Marines and officers. Most have had recent combat experience, with just a few of their ranks fresh to the Marine Corps. A weapons company serves to augment the warfighting capability of the three infantry line companies with specialized weapons and expertise. In the basic structure (called a table of organization, or T/O), a weapons company is composed, just like a line company, of three platoons. These three platoons, however, are differentiated by their weapons. The assault platoon employs missiles and rockets; the mortar platoon fires 81mm mortar systems; and the heavy-guns platoon uses M2 .50 caliber machine guns and MK-19 40mm automatic grenade launchers. Weapons companies provide extra firepower in support of line companies, depending on the mission.

Prior to deploying to Iraq, 2/3, based on 3/3's experiences, "retasked" the battalion's Weapons Company to function like a line company but to be more "mobile," or vehicle based. It temporarily renamed 2/3's Weapons Company "Whiskey Company," and the unit's individual platoons became MAPs, or Mobile Assault Platoons. This structure suited the battalion ideally.

After the initial weeks in Baghdadi, Whiskey was able to quickly occupy a position at Albu Hyatt, closer to the center of gravity in the Triad. Because the platoons were mobile, they were able to conduct operations throughout the expanse of desert to the south of Haditha, Haqlaniyah, and Barwana—a region used by Al Qaeda to hide weapons, hide themselves, and in some cases, plan operations and train for them. Whiskey, being mobile in nature, could quickly augment any of the line companies if needed. Furthermore, it helped hem in AQI during the insurgents' push for Haditha. The dam served as a natural blocking position to the north, and the MAPs of Whiskey kept Al Qaeda "pressed against the wall" in the south as Echo, Fox, and Golf hammered the organization in the core of the Triad.

As soon as Whiskey arrived in Baghdadi, it set up shop in the large military compound next to the resort complex. The company mission paralleled that of all other companies of 2/3: increase security in the region. A significant component involved working with the local IP and the Iraqi Army in the area. Whiskey would also conduct a number of daily patrols to root out any insurgent activity.

But disaster nearly struck almost immediately.

"Let's dismount and start sweeping," ordered First Lieutenant Patrick Kinser, Whiskey's executive officer, during one of the company's first missions. They patrolled along a key route that the Marines called MSR Bronze, or Main Supply Route Bronze. Bronze paralleled the Euphrates River corridor from the Baghdadi region up to the dam, and thus was a critical route for both the battalion and AQI.

Kinser, a veteran of 2/3's deployment to Afghanistan, where he served as an infantry platoon commander, maintained an aggressive outlook for his time in Iraq: he wanted to be as thorough as possible, to never see any of his patrols fall prey to an IED, and to uncover as many bombmaking components and enemy fabrication and planning cells as possible. With so much open desert in their company AO, and with AQI's attention focused on Haditha and surrounding areas, all in Whiskey knew that perhaps their greatest role in bolstering security would be to interdict IED proliferation. Kinser and others of Whiskey sought to shut down AQI's ability to create and emplace IEDs altogether.

After dismounting and dispersing, the Marines of Kinser's patrol swept a corridor centered along a dirt road that parallels Bronze just north of Baghdadi. Each Marine focused on every detail of the ground: every contour, every divot, every slight shadow, every bump, every miniscule detail. *Is that a wire or a twig? What's that trash bag doing out in the desert? Why are those rocks stacked atop each other?*

They all had trained hard for this. But nothing could substitute for actually being on scene in Iraq, where the slightest oversight could mean the end of a life—or lives—or the blasting away of limbs, sight, or hearing. They'd all seen images of victims of IEDs. Their faces a mass of shiny scar tissue. Their bodies missing one, two, three, even four limbs. Many had seen the horrors in person. Many knew those who suffered from these insidious weapons. They knew of stories of phantom pain. Of waking up in the middle of the night screaming, drenched in sweat, shaking uncontrollably.

They all had imagined loved ones seeing them for the first time recovering, and how they'd wince and turn away at the sight of disfigurement. With IEDs, one fraction of a second's oversight led to an unending nightmare for the remainder of the lives of survivors of the blast.

And they all had read about the seriousness of IEDs. Their superiors had lectured them, experts had coached them. After-action reports and battle summaries had given them insight and awareness. Prior to departing to Iraq, the lieutenant, like all those of Whiskey, pored over 3/3's after-action reports, intel reports, and other communications about enemy TTPs (tactics, techniques, and procedures) and equipment. Knowing that their lives depended on their knowledge, perception, and situational awareness, they had absorbed every detail.

Kinser even came up with his own "enemy" tactics, trying to think of any means that they might use, ones not yet employed. The enemy in the area being the most capable, battle hardened, most experienced of AQI, Kinser and others of Whiskey knew that they would continue to evolve and adapt their tactics and mechanisms to try to stay one step ahead of the Americans.

Kinser and the Marines in Whiskey had done their homework. But nothing instilled raw, intense focus like actually being there, step by step, knowing that each move forward could trigger the life-changing, blinding cloud of white followed immediately by unconsciousness.

Kinser walked along the tracks of an M1 Abrams that had recently driven on the road, looking for any telltale signs of one of those hidden killers—IEDs.

CLICK! The sound came from beneath Kinser's right boot. A stream of dust puffed into the air a few inches to the left. He froze.

"Hey, everyone," he calmly announced. "Back off from me. I think I might have just stepped on a pressure plate." The ground beneath his foot felt springy, not compressed like the ground leading up to it in the tank track.

"What's going on, sir?" one of Kinser's Marines asked.

"I heard a click, and the ground under my foot feels spongy."

"Well, if it was going to go off, then wouldn't it have gone off?"

"We don't know that," Kinser said. "It might go off when I release pressure on it, and then it might go off right under where you are standing. You know how they wire these things to be offset sometimes. So, get far back and be ready to call in EOD."

Maintaining pressure on the ground beneath his foot, Kinser leaned down and brushed away the sandy dirt around his boot. "It's an IED all right," he said as he found the first sign of a PIED, or package improvised explosive device. The unit was wrapped in plastic wrap, hence the spongy texture.

"Get way back and call EOD." He quickly but carefully unearthed the triggering mechanism, focusing more intensely than he ever had in his life. *Air trapped in the plastic wrap must have caused the puff of dust,* he thought. *But what about the click? Why aren't I dead, blown to a million bits?*

Then he found the power wires, each connected to a "spring" terminal on a six-volt battery. He built a mental image of how the basic circuit was wired but wondered if it could be a decoy. *Probably not, almost certainly not, but I don't want to find out.* Then he thought of another possibility: *I might have closed the circuit, but then maybe there is corrosion on one of the wires— and if I move the corroded wire, it will complete the circuit, and then it'll be all over.*

He pawed a moat around the triggering mechanism—working with a neurosurgeon's precision to not bump the wires in front of him. His fingertips slid over the cold metal of what felt like a line of artillery shells or possibly mortars, the business end of the IED.

"EOD is on its way, sir!" a Marine yelled.

"Thanks," Kinser said, then finished digging around the top of the device to see if there was any more to the circuit than he could initially determine. There wasn't.

"I'm not going to stand here like this until they get here. You guys get into a covered position," he ordered, then he carefully squeezed the wire attached to the positive terminal of the battery. "One, two," he mouthed. "Three."

He pulled the wire off the terminal and lifted his foot a tenth of a second later. He grabbed his M16, then carefully backed away from the IED, turned, and stepped only on the footsteps he had already indented into the ground on the way up to the device.

"Okay," he said to the Marines of his patrol. "Let's get some good standoff."

"You're the luckiest guy in Anbar," the EOD tech said after inspecting the device with a MARCbot and then in person. The pressure plate had been connected to four 152mm high-explosive artillery shells, daisy-chained together. "You completed the circuit, but the battery was dead. These guys know what they are doing, but got unlucky with their power source—lucky for you."

Kinser had discovered a new enemy tactic—they hid their own tracks, indenting them using wooden "stamps" to mimic the pattern of the M1A1's tread. It was a tactic that Kinser and other Whiskey Marines would keep an eye out for during the remainder of their deployment.

BOOM! EOD reduced the IED in place. A yellow fireball surged above the desert. The blast dissolved into the air, and then Kinser and his Marines continued their sweep.

A FEW DAYS later, members of Whiskey came upon another hidden IED. This time, however, luck was not on their side.

"Photograph the graffiti, Parnell," Sergeant Joshua Plunk instructed. They were on a patrol just outside the wire in Baghdadi. Plunk, who played a pivotal role as a mortarman during one of 2/3's major operations in Afghanistan, led a patrol that included Lance Corporal David Parnell, one of the few Whiskey Marines on his first combat tour. Plunk felt uneasy about the patrol. The streets, normally filled with people, were empty. The few residents they saw scurried away upon sighting the Marines. Furthermore, Plunk needed to pay extra attention to Parnell—the young Marine lacked what he felt to be a sufficient level of focus and attention to detail.

One day during pre-deployment training, Parnell, formally trained as a mortar forward observer, had been tasked with providing target grids during live fire mortar training. The rounds didn't impact slightly off target; they impacted hundreds of meters off target. Parnell had had the map upside down. Just after that live fire training, he committed what amounts to a cardinal sin for a junior Marine: he lost his Marine Corps identification card. Plunk always kept a watchful eye on Parnell.

As the lance corporal focused his camera on the pro-AQI graffiti, which Plunk noticed had been recently spray-painted on the wall, a man in the shadows a block away touched a wire to the terminal of a six-volt battery. BOOM! A huge explosion erupted from the wall. Plunk fell to the ground. A blazing hot chunk of steel had slashed into his right thigh, snapping his femur. Two IPs accompanying the patrol screamed in agony and rolled on the ground. Parnell couldn't feel his left hand. He reached for his M16—it was cut in half.

CRACK!—CRACK!—CRACK!—CRACK! From the shadows, five AQI ambushers emerged, one firing a PK machine gun, and the others sending bursts at the fallen patrol with AK-47s. Plunk rolled over, soaked in his own blood, and returned fire. A corpsman ran up to the sergeant as other Marines of the patrol took cover and returned fire. Other members of the IP, who had been trailing the lead elements of the patrol, began screaming as the rhythm of enemy gunfire slowed.

"They're gonna do the death blossom," one of the Marines yelled. "Stop!" he shouted to the IP. He turned to Plunk and the others. "Put your heads down!"

The IP formed a semicircle as the last of the enemy rounds snapped overhead and then clattered rounds off in most every direction—the Iraqi death blossom.

"Stop!" the Marine roared.

After about ten seconds of shooting, the death blossom ceased. The IPs then ran to their two injured compatriots. Plunk ordered a medevac for the two IPs, Parnell, and himself. Within minutes, a Dustoff had them en route to the trauma center at Al Asad.

Sergeant Plunk had taken the brunt of the explosion. He sustained not only a broken femur, but a concussion, a traumatic brain injury, and shrapnel wounds throughout his body. Once stabilized, doctors at Al Asad sent both Plunk and Parnell to Landstuhl, and then once they were recovered from surgery, arranged for them to return to the United States for further rehabilitation. Parnell accepted his US reassignment, but Plunk insisted he return to his fellow Whiskey Marines in Iraq. Months later, Plunk arrived back in Al Asad. He limped, but he was ready to get back in the fight.

Parnell would fully recover as well. However, during his rehabilitation, he made international news, in a way that seemingly contradicted his recovery.

A week after the explosion, Major Keven Matthews, 2/3's executive officer, called Lieutenant Kinser with a puzzling question: "Why is it that Al Qaeda is claiming that they have beheaded Lance Corporal David Parnell?"

Kinser had no answer. He had only received word that Parnell was recovering.

"A photo of his identification card is on extremist websites as proof that they captured him," Matthews continued. "His mother is freaking out. It's on the news all over the world."

A brief investigation followed. Parnell, after he lost his identification card and the Marine Corps replaced it, found the original. He didn't report that he had found it, however, and carried both with him. When the IED detonated, the blast flung the card he carried in his shoulder pocket into the air. Recovered by AQI, they used it as evidence of his capture.

11

══ ★ ══

MIRRORS OF TRUST AND DECEIT

THE HAIR ON THE BACK OF CAPTAIN PETE CAPUZZI'S NECK STOOD on end. He imagined his skin crawling. Capuzzi, the commander of Whiskey Company, stood before Colonel Sha'aban, the chief of the Baghdadi IP, and his deputy, Lieutenant Colonel Al-Asadi.

As AQI hit Whiskey with IEDs, ambushes, and mortar attacks—and it hit back—the company worked to establish a relationship with the local IP to foster enduring security in the Baghdadi area. First, however, they needed to gain a solid understanding of the key personalities in the police force, and friendly conversation would help establish that rapport.

"Tell me about your children," Sha'aban asked. "What are they like? How many daughters do you have?"

Capuzzi grinned briefly at Sha'aban during this first meeting. He didn't like anything about the colonel. But he needed to work with him. 3/3 had worked with Sha'aban and the Iraqi Army contingent in Baghdadi, and it had made steady, strong progress with both groups in the overall fight for security. Capuzzi and the Marines of Whiskey sought the same trajectory. But that didn't mean that he would trust Sha'aban, or like him.

Like Colonel Farouk, Sha'aban hailed from a Sunni Muslim tribe. Unlike Farouk, he wasn't from the town where he commanded the police force. Sha'aban was from Ramadi, over fifty miles distant from Baghdadi. There, his police work in Ramadi had impressed Colonel Blake Crowe, the commander of RCT-7, and others in senior military leadership positions, which ultimately brought him to Baghdadi.

Lieutenant Kinser had also held a great deal of mistrust of Sha'aban. He had been told about all the "good work" Sha'aban had done in Ramadi. "Whatever 'good work' means," Kinser said. "I suppose he's better than Al Qaeda, but probably not much better."

Despite their misgivings, Captain Capuzzi and the Whiskey Marines worked with Sha'aban, but they made far less progress in the Baghdadi region than Echo did working with Farouk and his IP in Haditha. The two IP groups stood far apart, not only geographically but also contextually and historically. The IP force in Baghdadi, the Marines learned, engaged in extortion as much as they did in security. This relationship stretched back to the earliest days of the Saddam Hussein regime's construction of the Baghdadi resort and military compound—outsiders with power over locals. Although Sunni, most IP weren't from the area. Poorly paid, they sought to supplement their income through shakedowns of the populace.

While they bullied the locals of Baghdadi, the IP was cowed by the threat of AQI. Just over a year before Whiskey arrived in Baghdadi, AQI had captured eight IP of the area. Like they had done to the police in Haditha, the terrorists tortured and then decapitated the officers. As a message to the locals and the other IP, they hung the headless, naked, and slashed bodies from light poles in the center of the city.

"SOMEONE SHOT SHA'ABAN," Kinser reported to Captain Capuzzi. It was just over a week since the relief-in-place with 3/3. "Out in the middle of the desert."

"What do you mean the middle of the desert?" Capuzzi asked. "Everywhere out here is in the middle of the desert."

"I mean, like, in the middle of the desert," Kinser replied. "Not on a main road, not on a dirt road, not on any road at all. Out in the middle of the desert," he paused briefly. "The middle of nowhere."

"I don't get it," Capuzzi responded. "Who is he with? Is he being medevac-ed?"

"He just called it in," Kinser responded. "Sha'aban just called it in himself with a sat[ellite] phone. All we know right now is that he's been shot." Kinser paused. "Or at least that's what he's saying." Minutes later, Kinser learned more about the situation. "Lieutenant Colonel Al-Asadi was with him."

"Was?" Capuzzi responded. "You mean *is,* right?"

"No, sir," Kinser responded, "*was.* He's dead. Shot in the head. Sha'aban took a wound to his left shoulder and he's driving back himself."

"They were out there all alone!" Capuzzi exclaimed. "All alone, just those two. No other IP, no Marines, nobody but those two. Al-Asadi gets shot in the head and Sha'aban just gets wounded in the shoulder?"

BOOM! An explosion sent concussive shockwaves through the military compound.

"One-twenties," Kinser said at the distinctive sound of the football-sized 120mm mortars used by AQI.

BOOM! The second round hit closer to the Whiskey COC. "They're walking them in on us."

CRACK! IP personnel scrambled for cover in the compound. CRACK! The fourth round landed inside the wire. The explosion hurled shrapnel in all directions. An IP officer buckled and fell to the ground, convulsing in agony. In less than a minute, corpsmen attached to Whiskey had the IP stabilized and Dust-off crews at Al Asad spun up an air ambulance Black Hawk. The IP had a patrol tearing out of the compound within minutes of learning that their number one and number two had been attacked.

CLACK!—CLACK!—CLACK!—CLACK! Machine gun fire ripped into their three-vehicle convoy moments after the IP sped out of the wire. AQI rounds slammed into the lead vehicles. Volleys of RPGs followed. The IP skidded their trucks to a halt and jumped onto the pavement. Another death blossom bloomed in the streets of Baghdadi, then silence. One of the IPs lay curled up on the ground, hit by fire from the ambush.

"This seems too coincidental," Capuzzi fumed minutes later. He and Kinser worked up a Dustoff medevac for the wounded officer. "Like clockwork," the captain said.

Sha'aban arrived an hour later. Kinser, some of his Marines, and a contingent of the Baghdadi IP inspected the car. Corpsmen inspected Sha'aban and the corpse of Lieutenant Colonel Al-Asadi. "Al-Asadi was shot in the head," Kinser reported to Capuzzi. "No doubt about that. Shot to the back of his head."

"And Sha'aban?" Capuzzi asked.

"A grazing wound at best," Kinser answered. "Like a scrape. On his shoulder. Not sure it was even caused by a bullet."

"And so just one gunshot to Al-Asadi?" the company commander asked.

"Right," Kinser smirked. "And just the scrape on Sha'aban's shoulder." Kinser paused, rolling his eyes. "He's claiming that a bunch of masked guys stopped them and shot them from outside the car, then took off. Problem with that story is that there are no bullet holes anywhere on the car." Capuzzi shook his head. "And now Sha'aban wants to get medevac-ed to Al Asad."

"For his scrape?" Capuzzi asked.

"Yeah. He needs to recover, all right," Kinser laughed. "He just wants those Al Asad chicken wings." Kinser arranged a ground medevac for Sha'aban, then set out to finish planning for an upcoming operation that would occur the following night.

THE OPERATION, WHICH would combine the forces of Whiskey Company Marines, the local contingent of the Iraqi Army, and the Baghdadi IP, was to take place at Albu Hyatt, the small town that Whiskey would call home after their time in Baghdadi. It was a "cordon and search" mission, where the forces would loosely encircle the village with blocking positions at key routes and passageways in and out. The mission would be the first time the Whiskey Marines visited the small, typically quiet hamlet. Intelligence for the operation had come from Sha'aban.

"So, we'll see how it goes," Kinser told Capuzzi. "And now we're adding 'find who shot Al-Asadi' to our list of mission goals."

"I think we already know, Kinser," Capuzzi said.

CRACK! A SINGLE gunshot rang out late the next night in Albu Hyatt. Kinser was one of just eight Marines at the village that night; the majority of the force consisted of Baghdadi IP officers and Iraqi Army soldiers. The lieutenant was with his interpreter, Joe, asking a local man questions about possible AQI activity in the region when the gunshot split into the night.

"Let's go," he said to his 'terp. Originally from the Iraqi city of Najaf, Joe, whose actual name is Dhurgham, spent years in Saddam Hussein's army and spent time in Anbar. The Marines would come to trust not only his communication skills but also his sense about individuals and situations.

"This isn't too good, Lieutenant Kinser," Joe said as the two stepped outside. The scene before them was frenetic. A sea of IP swarmed about on a dirt road leading to a rise above the shore of the Euphrates. Two masked IP officers approached Kinser and Joe. They raised their hands, palms out, and made pushing gestures at the two.

"All good!" one announced. "All good!"

"Ask them what's going on, Joe," Kinser said. The interpreter and the two spoke tersely in Arabic.

"He says that someone accidentally fired his gun. He says there's no problem."

"Yeah, right," Kinser replied. The lieutenant forced his way past the two AK-47-wielding IPs, pushing one to the side.

"NO! NO! NO!" one of them yelled at Kinser.

"Come on, Joe," Kinser said.

"These guys are getting crazy, Lieutenant Kinser!"

"It's all crazy." With Joe close behind him, Kinser pushed through a crowd of IP. A few steps later he stood on the edge of the small bluff. Below him, a man lay crumbled, his hands bound behind his back. Blood from the man's side streamed down the dirt slope. Kinser jumped down next to him. He rolled him over and his intestines fell onto the desert floor. He'd been shot in the back at close range. He wasn't a man, but a boy, probably fourteen or fifteen. The boy's eyes bulged toward Patrick when he rolled him over. His body convulsed. "Joe!" Kinser yelled. "Get a doctor!" A corpsman appeared seconds later.

"Nothing we can do," the doc said to Kinser. "He's dead."

POP! POP! POP! Kinser sprang up and climbed to the top of the bluff. The crowd of IP had become more agitated. POP! "Over there, Joe." Kinser pointed to a nearby house with another crowd of IP outside. The lieutenant barged through the front door to see Captain Capuzzi screaming at an IP officer who held a pistol at his side.

"The IP think this man's son had something to do with the incident with Colonel Sha'aban yesterday," Capuzzi said to Kinser. "They took the son away for questioning, and I'm trying to figure out where he's at." Capuzzi paused. "I came over when I heard the gunshots—they're trying to intimidate the family into admitting their son or they had something to do with the shooting by firing into the ceiling."

"His son is dead," Kinser said calmly. "They bound him and shot him in the back down by the river. Threw him off a bluff." Kinser and Capuzzi hustled the IP out of the home as Joe explained what happened. The man wailed at the loss of his son. "What an introduction to Albu Hyatt," Kinser said to Captain Capuzzi.

"This is going to be a long deployment," the company commander responded. "Let's get control of all these IP."

Before they had departed for Anbar Province in Iraq, the Marines of Whiskey had learned about all the tribal infighting that occurred. However, witnessing such brutality and horror brought both anger and intense compassion. *Who could the father trust?* Kinser pondered. *He can't call the police for the murder of his son—they are the ones who murdered him. Would he ever trust the Marines? We came up here with the IP. Would he be complicit with Al Qaeda? Is he part of AQI? Or is he someone who just wants to be left alone but is caught in the middle of a never-ending struggle for power?*

For Whiskey, it was also a never-ending struggle.

12

★

COIN AND THE
JUMP COMMAND POST

ALTHOUGH IT WAS OFFICIALLY DESIGNATED THE HEADQUARTERS (doctrinally called the "command post" or just "CP") for the battalion during 2/3's deployment, Lieutenant Colonel Jim Donnellan rarely spent time at Haditha Dam. Upon arrival in the AO, he and his staff established the "Forward CP" at Echo's FOB in Haditha, as it was the battalion's main area of effort. Though Donnellan (usually) slept at the Forward CP, he spent most of his days and nights outside the wire, in his mobile command post, or "Jump CP." Always accompanied by Sergeant Major Patrick Wilkinson, Donnellan and the Jump typically spent from five to seven days per week moving through the entire area of operations. They regularly visited all company forward operating bases, police stations, Iraqi Army bases, and the numerous small entry control points and vehicle control points (ECPs and VCPs) scattered throughout the region. They participated in combat operations large and small, and met with local governmental, business, and tribal leaders. The Jump, typically a small convoy of Humvees and sometimes a seven-ton, also did its part to rid the area of IEDs—sweeping for them, often discovering them, and, on a few occasions, hitting them.

From a technical standpoint, the battalion's collective fight was composed of a continuous, fluid series of "distributed operations"—multiple simultaneous discrete combat operations and patrols undertaken by individual units throughout the entire AO. These operations included the meet-and-greets, MEDCAPS (Medical Capability Missions, providing medicine and basic healthcare to the local citizenry), raids, scout sniper operations, training of IP and Iraqi Army, civil affairs operations, convoys, intelligence gathering, daily patrols, and more. Although each unit, from squad to company, planned and executed these missions, Donnellan and Wilkinson always had overall situational awareness (SA) on each mission, whether they were at the Forward CP or the Jump CP. Technology connected all components of the warfighting effort through encrypted radios, unmanned aircraft systems (UAS) feed, and the Blue Force Tracker, or BFT, which shows, in real time, where individual units are located and their status. All of this information flow and interconnectivity allowed for solid, consistent, uninterrupted command-and-control, or C2—and it all could be monitored right from the seat of Donnellan's Humvee.

The mobile nature of the Jump also allowed for invaluable face time with his company commanders, their lieutenants, and the Marines themselves. Donnellan's decades of Marine Corps leadership and his time as battalion commander in Afghanistan (a very distributed battlespace, much more so than in Iraq) instilled in him the critical importance of not only in-person visits but also actual participation with Marines during their operations. Donnellan and Wilkinson's mobility and frequent appearances around the AO were especially effective in their work with Matt Tracy, the Haditha IP, and local leaders in Haditha.

Their active, on-the-ground command was an ideal complement to the finely tuned counterinsurgency campaign they waged. Donnellan didn't seek to micromanage or to "look over the shoulder of" his subordinates. To the contrary, he sought guidance from his subordinates on how he and his staff could further enable their counterinsurgency fight, particularly in Haditha. The goal was always to leave the AO in a state of victory—with AQI defeated, local infrastructure restored, and an enduring peace built on a strong and lasting indigenous security force and a burgeoning economy. Donnellan took the fight for the Triad personally and leaned heavily on his experience in Afghanistan, where he had also waged a counterinsurgency campaign. That experience oriented him toward a more pragmatic approach than a theoretical one.

"Like it or not, the locals see us as an invading force," he explained, "and we have to go a lot further than your brain might want to think it will go to engender trust in the local populace." Like Tracy, Donnellan focused on the betterment of the situation of the population. "The only tactic that I thought had any hope for success was the real, traditional full-on COIN mindset, where you are protecting the people, with the center of gravity for the long-term goals being the police."

He further explained the counterinsurgency mindset: "It isn't a clean 'us versus them.' There are no front lines. The enemy doesn't wear a uniform, and the fight isn't for ground, it is for the population—not to subjugate them or 'win them over,' but for the local people to be able to take ownership of their future and reject oppression by an outside force."

Donnellan, like others intimately familiar with the situation on the ground in Iraq, understood that, like the Taliban in Afghanistan, AQI was an invading force in Iraq. Its members may have paid locals, who were impoverished and desperate to feed their families as a result of the actions of Al Qaeda and the war in general, to act as temporary appendages to its movement. Simple employment, however, isn't indicative of ideological alignment. AQI was an outside invading force, not an uprising endemic to the country or to the region.

During pre-deployment training and, most importantly, during his visits to the Marines in the Triad during his rounds in the Jump, the battalion commander emphasized that the Marines were to conduct themselves with selflessness, empathy, and understanding for and alignment with the local population. "We never wanted to hear the Marines say, 'these people' or 'they don't understand' or 'they don't appreciate what we're doing.' That's a dangerous mindset. It defeats a COIN campaign from within."

Like Tracy, Donnellan stressed that their mission inherently subsumed the safety of the Iraqi population over their own. "But our guys got it," Donnellan said of his Marines. "It was not theoretical for them. They were picking up pieces of a buddy, putting them in a Ziploc, going to a memorial, and then going out on a patrol the next day—or sometimes a few hours later—and treating the population with respect, seeking to protect them, because they knew it isn't the population that did this to their buddy, but an enemy that hides behind the population and blends in and camouflages itself with the people."

Both he and Wilkinson sought, from the very first day, to instill this mindset throughout the entire battalion during its deployment. "That's the reason we were so aggressive about traveling the battlespaces. We had to keep the mantra going. You can't let any of the Marines ever get even the slightest victim mentality, or feel sorry for themselves, or want to hunker down and stop going into certain areas of their AO because they'd fear it to be too dangerous."

Donnellan also noted the importance of understanding that COIN is personality based. "It is much harder than it briefs. And we, the United States Military, make it much harder than it should be. If you form teams based on personality and how they'll conduct classic counterinsurgency, then you can create more synergy and a little less friction just by how you organize the battlespace." Hence his selection of Matt Tracy for the battalion's main effort, in Haditha.

Donnellan also repeated to the battalion that their fight was not a new style of combat. "On my desk in Afghanistan I had a copy of *The Small Wars Manual* [an official Marine Corps publication about the undertaking of smaller guerrilla and counterinsurgency campaigns]—the old version, not the new version—and it gives a great historical context of the Marine Corps and modern counterinsurgency. Throughout Marine Corps history, that's been one of our specialties, small wars and counterinsurgency. In Haditha we were just carrying on that tradition."

Donnellan recognized that media portrayals overlooked that important component of Marine Corps capability and legacy, however. "If you are a young Marine, and the extent of your exposure is to episodes like Iwo Jima, Guadalcanal, and Chosin, then you think that is all we do—the big wars. But the Marine Corps has a tremendous history in counterinsurgency, leading foreign militaries, building up police forces, and Wilkinson and I talked about that repeatedly with the Marines, during training and then once in Iraq."

During their frequent visits to the FOBs and the Marines of all the battalion's companies, Donnellan and Wilkinson paid close attention to each and every Marine. "We looked for any change in mindset, whether it was shown through body language or actual language," the battalion commander explained.

A phrase we looked out for was "we need to take the gloves off"—and I had to bite my lip. I didn't want to shoot the Marine down. We wanted people to be true believers in this intricate style of warfare, and not just comply to guidelines we set forth. I wanted to make sure that they were all believers, not that they were just going to comply because they felt that they were being watched all the time. So when I heard "take the gloves off," I'd bite my lip and I'd ask, "What does that mean? What does it mean to take the gloves off? Does it mean cutting heads off like AQI? Work with us and not Al Qaeda because we're more badass than they are?" We weren't on a mission to out-intimidate AQI. We didn't even want to accidentally detain the wrong person. If you grab a local man, arrest him, drag him off, and he is completely innocent, then anyone on the fence between us and AQI will be that much more favorable to Al Qaeda when they see that, particularly the man and his family members. It's COIN math—arrest one wrong person, and then you just gave the enemy four or five new converts to their cause.

Just as the pace of activity for individual Marines in each of 2/3's companies began explosively and then continued to ratchet ever higher with each footstep in the deployment, so did the tempo for Donnellan and his staff. The fabric of the battalion's overall mission, cohesive from the start, tightened ever more as the Jump CP threaded across its myriad components. While always maintaining constant C2 over the entire battalion, Donnellan and Sergeant Major Wilkinson bolstered the resolve of individual Marines, fire teams, squads, platoons, and entire companies with their invaluable frequent personal visits throughout the AO. A strict pragmatist, Lieutenant Colonel Donnellan saw himself as a mission enabler above any other role. He was there to support the Marines and the mission itself.

Arguably the most coveted and admired role in the Marine Corps, infantry battalion commander (notably, one who is deployed to a combat theater, particularly a battlespace as active as the Haditha Triad) ranks as one of the most difficult, if not the most difficult, in the service. Responsible for over eleven hundred personnel in one of the most violent, dangerous, and unpredictable places in modern history, and in an ever-restrictive command environment under RCT-7, Donnellan fought daily to keep his task force driving toward victory. An incredibly strong staff, notably his operations officer, or OpsO, Major Joseph "Trane" McCloud, allowed Donnellan to spend so much time outside the wire, maintaining forward mission progress.

In addition to his direct support of the Marines on the ground, Donnellan met regularly with Colonel Farouk and his IP, trying, with Matt Tracy, to keep that vital component of the effort on track. A single misstep from Farouk could derail the entire mission. Through his interpreter and cultural advisor "Big John," Donnellan also met with local sheiks and talked with prospective local civic leaders. He hoped to have an operational government in Haditha up and running long before the battalion's departure—but in the early days, as mortars rained down, ambushes erupted, IEDs exploded, and the local population remained in the shadows, that goal seemed far beyond the horizon.

Nevertheless, working with Matt Tracy and the other company commanders, Sergeant Major Wilkinson, Trane McCloud, and key figures in Haditha, Donnellan could foresee a possible, even likely "Haditha Awakening." But every aspect of the battalion, every component of the fight needed to drive forward, and he made sure he did his part in leading this progress with his consistent visits throughout the AO with the Jump. He led, like Captain Tracy, very much from the front.

Then there was Colonel Crowe. Just as the pressure from AQI increased daily, so did Crowe's micromanagement, according to Donnellan and Tracy.

Crowe, the son of Admiral William J. Crowe, the Chairman of the Joint Chiefs of Staff during the Reagan administration, seemed to verbally reprimand Marines for any and every infraction. Ron Gridley said they saw Crowe personally tear through a Marine's rucksack and inspect gear, even at the most inappropriate moment.

Crowe also kept constant watch over the various companies in the Triad. He did this with UAS (unmanned aircraft systems), commonly called "drones." RCT-7 operated a small fleet of low-altitude unmanned aircraft that provided Crowe with a continuous video feed of activity throughout the Triad. He also monitored radio nets used by the battalion. As soon as he or a member of his staff noticed something that struck them as objectionable, Crowe or his staff would contact the battalion with questions. "It was such a nightmare, with all the responsibilities that [Donnellan] had, and all that he wanted to get done, to have to deal with Crowe," Wilkinson said. "As if the situation couldn't get any tougher with all that AQI was throwing at us, Donnellan had to contend with Crowe and his constant nitpicking and threats."

But the battalion commander and Wilkinson didn't allow the interference to hinder their progress. Crowe represented just one more hurdle that the two used to demonstrate unflinching leadership under fire—fire from every direction, at all hours of the day and night.

The most taxing duty for Lieutenant Colonel Donnellan was the gut-wrenching task that followed deadly AQI strikes: contacting the families of those killed and injured. Because Donnellan, Wilkinson, and the Jump spent so much time outside the wire, all throughout 2/3's AO, the lieutenant colonel understood the hardships the Marines faced. He knew the ground situation intimately. He knew the smell of a firefight, the surprise of a tossed grenade, the lay of individual neighborhoods, the looks that locals would sometimes throw at the Marines. He understood the incredible adversity, austerity, and intense frustration his Marines faced. He also knew the devastation wrought on the Marines when one of their ranks fell victim to an IED attack, an ambush, a mortar detonation, a tossed hand grenade, or a sniper strike.

Despite all of his responsibilities in supporting the fight, he always made time to contact family members to offer condolences and to discuss the role the Marines played and the importance of their mission. Both he and Sergeant Major Wilkinson maintained an unflinching exterior, despite devastation. As the deployment continued, however, tragedy would dog the Marines of 2/3.

Fisheye view of the Haditha Dam at dusk.

Silhouette of an Echo Company Marine during a patrol in the city of Haditha.

Typical scene of an Echo Company patrol in the city of Haditha.

A Fox Company
Marine during a
patrol in Barwana,
inspecting some
disturbed ground
for signs of a
buried improvised
explosive device.

The Euphrates River
at dusk, photographed
from the roof of the
Whiskey Company
forward operating base,
Albu Hyatt.

An Echo Company Marine pours diesel fuel into a "burn shitter," part of the daily routine at the Echo Company forward operating base in the city of Haditha.

A Whiskey Company Marine patrols along the shore of the Euphrates River, framed by fronds of palm trees, Albu Hyatt.

Lieutenant Colonel
James E. "Jim" Donnellan
during a patrol in the city
of Haditha.

Members of the Iraqi Police
with a detained suspected Al
Qaeda member on the outskirts
of the city of Haditha.

"Complacency Kills," a mantra repeated by members of the battalion throughout the entirety of their deployment to the Triad.

A sign at the Golf Company forward operating base in Haqlaniyah graphically showing why all needed to be fully "geared up" (wearing their personal protective equipment—flak jacket, Kevlar helmet, goggles, etc.) at all times when outside of a fortified building at the base. All company forward operating bases came under near constant attack for the first months of the deployment, including by mortars, like exploded ones hanging beneath the sign.

An MTVR, or Medium Tactical Vehicle Replacement, AKA a "seven-ton," fitted with a mine roller, during a combat operation north of the city of Haditha.

A Whiskey Company Marine searches the trunk of a sedan for possible explosives or weapons. The nature of "the fight" was such that anyone could be a potential enemy or suicide bomber.

Whiskey Company Marines inspect a bridge in which members of Al Qaeda frequently emplaced improvised explosive devices, carefully searching for any signs around a crater from a recent, deadly blast.

Whiskey Company Marines return to the Albu Hyatt forward operating base in an MTVR, or Medium Tactical Vehicle Replacement, a "seven-ton," fitted with a mine roller.

Members of the battalion met daily with locals during their patrols. They were there for the people, to drive out Al Qaeda and help them reestablish a safe, prosperous society.

Lieutenant Brian Park, a platoon commander in Whiskey Company, takes notes from a local during a patrol outside of Albu Hyatt.

(Left) Corporal James Steuter, an Echo Company Marine, speaks with a local as children look on during a patrol on the outskirts of the city of Haditha.

(Facing page, top) Captain Matt Tracy during a meeting with local leaders of the city of Haditha.

(Facing page, middle) Members of the Iraqi Police with whom the battalion worked closely in their successful counterinsurgency campaign.

(Facing page, bottom) A member of the battalion checks captured Al Qaeda terrorists awaiting transport to a detention facility.

One of the many weapons caches discovered by the battalion during their successful deployment.

Two Marine Corps AV-8B II Harriers approach a Marine Corps KC-130J to refuel during a close air support mission high over the desert of the Al Anbar Province of Iraq, near Haditha. Marine aviation assets, based out of Al Asad Airbase, proved invaluable to 2/3 during their deployment to the Haditha Triad.

Marines at the firing range during their deployment to the Haditha Triad.

Sergeant Jason Tarr, an Echo Company Marine, scans the distance during a patrol in the city of Haditha.

A Golf Company mounted patrol on the dusty, narrow city streets of Haqlaniyah.

An Echo Company Marine takes aim during a firefight.

"Lioness" Marines at the Golf Company forward operating base in Haqlaniyah. Lionesses proved invaluable to 2/3's efforts.

An M1A1 Abrams main battle tank during a Fox Company patrol in Barwana.

Gunnery Sergeant "Gunny" Terry Elliott at the Albu Hyatt Whiskey Company forward operating base just prior to embarking on a patrol.

Mike Scholl in October 2005 in the Hindu Kush of eastern Kunar Province during 2/3's Afghanistan deployment, just over a year before an Al Qaeda IED killed him on the outskirts of the city of Haditha.

Aerial view of the Euphrates River and the pontoon bridge that connected Haditha (upper part of photograph) with Barwana (lower part of photograph). The IED that killed Mario Gonzalez, Timothy Brown, and Mike Scholl was emplaced just inside the dogleg bend in the road leading away from the bridge on the Haditha side of the river.

Sergeant Major Patrick Wilkinson, the battalion's sergeant major, during a combat operation north of the city of Haditha, flanked by two Marines of the battalion.

A young Iraqi boy smiles at an Echo Company Marine during a patrol in the city of Haditha. Members of the battalion were hailed as liberators and saviors of the population for their incredible dedication and fidelity to their mission of defeating Al Qaeda and restoring peace to the region.

Locals greet a Fox Company Marine during a patrol on the outskirts of Barwana. When the battalion arrived in the Triad, locals rarely emerged due to the oppression of Al Qaeda. By the end of the deployment, Marines of the battalion couldn't walk more than a block without locals approaching them, some in tears, thanking them for returning the area to normalcy.

Young Iraqi children smile and laugh with a Fox Company Marine during a patrol in Barwana. Images like these illustrate just how great a victory 2/3's proved to be.

13

GLIMMERS AND DARKNESS

"I'M A FATHER!" TWENTY-ONE-YEAR-OLD MIKE SCHOLL PROUDLY announced just a few days after the deaths of Jeremy Sandvick Monroe and Derek Jones. The moment was a brief highlight amid the depths of anguish. Scholl's wife, Melissa, had given birth to a healthy daughter, Addison. "I can't wait to meet her in person!" he said repeatedly to others in the FOB, including Mario Anes, James Steuter, Nic Carson, and Captain Tracy. Everyone in the company celebrated and congratulated Scholl, a tough but soft-spoken member of the battalion who had participated in some of the most grueling operations in the mountains of the Hindu Kush during 2/3's Afghan deployment.

On a satellite phone, Scholl asked Melissa to hold the speaker up to Addison so that he could hear some of his daughter's first "words." His wife then held the phone to Addison's ear. Scholl spoke so she could hear his voice, a half world distant.

He called whenever time allowed, again and again, even if only to speak to Melissa and hear Addison for just a minute. He counted the months, weeks, and days until he would return to Hawaii and reunite with them. He thought of the future:

birthday parties, vacations, Saturdays at the beach, first days at school. Melissa emailed photographs of her and Addison in her hospital bed and then their first days back at home. Scholl showed them off to all in Echo.

Other members of the battalion also looked forward to returning home to new additions. Thirty-four-year-old Gunnery Sergeant Terry Elliott, of Whiskey Company, awaited his firstborn, due in November. Twenty-three-year-old Second Lieutenant Josh Booth, an Echo Company platoon commander on his first combat tour, had recently welcomed a daughter, Gracie, to the world, sister to their firstborn, Tristan, a boy.

DESPITE THE GLIMMERS of elation rooted in thoughts of first encounters with newborns and reunions with loved ones, the Marines maintained stalwart focus in the ever-present shroud of darkness AQI cast over the AO. "There's still at least one sniper out there!" Captain Tracy bellowed, memories of McClellan and Jeremy Sandvick Monroe piercing his thoughts. Insurgents continued to ramp up their attacks in Haditha, Haqlaniyah, Barwana, and Baghdadi. "Now they're paying local children a hundred dollars to toss a grenade at Marines!" Tracy announced the newly discovered tactic. "It's another cheap way for AQI to turn the people of Haditha against us—they're trying to get us to suspect all children of being grenade throwers, in hopes we start killing the children of the city."

The Marines didn't fall for the ruse. Tracy and Donnellan, in meetings with local Haditha leaders, explained that they saw this as an early sign of AQI's desperation in the face of 2/3's resolute posture.

Only a handful of children threw grenades at Marines. None of the "attacks" caused any injuries. None killed. The Marines maintained composure and restraint, their trigger fingers straight throughout each incident.

Then AQI tried a new tactic in Haditha to try to turn the population against 2/3: killing local children and blaming the Americans for the murders.

"Doc Opie!" Corporal John Hunsberger yelled, bursting into the Echo FOB. In his arms he carried a six-year-old girl, blood pouring from her head. His squad had come across her father kneeling over her. AQI had shot the girl, not knowing that her father watched the event unfold and that Hunsberger's squad was approaching. Hunsberger and his squad had found the girl in the street after an ambush. The Marines couldn't return fire because the Al Qaeda fighters hid behind locals. The AQI members vanished, leaving the girl in their wake, presumably in an attempt to place blame on the Americans for her wound. The Marines rushed her back to the FOB.

Navy Hospital Corpsman Phillip "Doc Opie" Oppliger was waiting and immediately went to work to try to stabilize her. Her wound was so severe, however, he realized that his attempts were in vain. But she was so young. He fought to save her—he did anything he could to save the young Iraqi girl.

"Come on!" a Marine yelled at Doc Opie. "Bird's inbound!" Oppliger, cradling the bleeding girl, ran out to the main gate of Echo's FOB. He climbed with her into the back of a seven-ton, then motioned to a Marine to head to the LZ. The Dustoff roared overhead just as the seven-ton skidded to a halt in the soccer field.

Doc Opie and the medics of the Dustoff knew the likely outcome. She'd been shot in the head. They fought valiantly to save her. But by the time the bird landed at Al Asad, she had breathed her last breath.

JUST BECAUSE AQI had a new tactic didn't mean it ceased using old ones, however. As Captain Tracy mentioned, at least one of the snipers remained at large—at least one.

Lance Corporal Max Draper checked his watch: 1500 hours—three in the afternoon. "This is a late start," Draper said to his fire team. A machine gunner, Draper was a fire team leader in Echo Company's 3rd Platoon, commanded by Second Lieutenant Josh Booth.

Draper, a veteran of 2/3's Afghan deployment, couldn't help but compare his time in the Hindu Kush with this deployment in Haditha. Afghanistan had been physically exhausting and miserable, with all the long-distance foot mobile movements. Haditha, however, was mentally and emotionally miserable. By that day, the seventeenth of October, Draper had been in dozens of firefights throughout Haditha. The pattern was always the same. His squad would get "lit up," usually from the palm groves, then the Marines would identify the shooters and "dump rounds" into their positions. Then the AQI attackers would turn tail and flee.

As Draper left the wire that day with his squad, he carried his mental preparations and training along with him, walking cautiously. His steps marked the first of a multiday patrol for him and his squad. Most of the patrols to that point had lasted three to four hours. This would be three days and take his squad down along "Boardwalk"—the name the Marines had bestowed on the road that ran parallel to the Euphrates, adjacent to the palm groves. Their objective was to escort Marine Corps Combat Engineers around the outskirts of Haditha.

Draper didn't know the reason for the engineers' presence. Nobody in his squad knew. They would soon find out, however, that this patrol was the very beginning of a plan hatched by Jim Donnellan and Major Trane McCloud—a plan that the battalion commander and his operations officer were implementing as a critical component of a greater strategy to decisively win the AO.

Draper and the other Marines of his squad took one carefully placed step after another. Dispersed and keeping watch over the engineers, they readied themselves for any eventuality—most likely a spray of AK-47 rounds from the "jungle," what they all called the palm groves.

As the engineers took photographs and notes, Draper and the others of his squad studied every detail of the groves, looking for any movement. Draper located a mound of earth and knelt down next to it. Carrying an M249 SAW (squad automatic weapon), he set the gun up on its bipod at the top of a hump, then scanned the distance through the sights. In Afghanistan he had carried an M240 medium machine gun that fired a 7.62mm round. Draper loved the two-forty, but in Haditha it would have been "sniper bait," so he patrolled with the smaller, less-conspicuous SAW, which fires a 5.56mm round—less powerful than the 7.62 bullet but good enough to do the job.

"Take cover!" Draper yelled. He saw the first muzzle flash of the ambush before anyone heard the CRACK!—CRACK!—CRACK! of the AK-47 rounds heading toward them. *BRRRR-RRRRRRRRRR!* Draper unleashed a ten-shot burst of rounds in the direction of the initial muzzle flash. An "area weapon," the SAW fires rounds that disperse as they leave the muzzle, creating a swath, not a point, of fire to suppress an enemy.

Behind Draper, Marines of his squad then fired "well-placed rounds" at the enemy position with M16s. The tried-and-true infantry tactic relies on the SAW to get the enemy to "break contact" (stop firing) because of the barrage of incoming rounds and then hits the enemy using the more precise M16 fire.

Just as the first volley of Draper's fire tore into the enemy position, two more AQI fighters opened up on them. Knowing that this was likely the first of many firefights of the patrol, Draper took care to conserve his rounds. He made each burst count.

The firefight continued for another thirty seconds—about average—then the three fighters broke contact and ran.

"Everyone okay?" Draper yelled, looking around. "Anybody hit?" All, including the combat engineers, had made it through the ambush unscathed. Draper and the other Marines of his squad jumped up to gauge the egress route, or getaway path, of the enemy fighters. "Long gone by now, probably on a boat." Draper referred to a common enemy tactic: after an ambush, the enemy would turn and run, often to the shore of the Euphrates to a waiting boat, where they would hide their weapons—they knew that the Marines could not shoot unless they had PID, or positive identification, of hostile intent. No weapons out, no PID, free to go.

The ambush demonstrated what Major McCloud and Lieutenant Colonel Donnellan had identified as the mission-critical component to all enemy attacks: the egress route. No egress route, no ambush. And that, Draper and the other Marines of the patrol would eventually learn, was the purpose of escorting the combat engineers.

CRACK!—CRACK!—CRACK! More AK-47 fire followed just minutes later. Draper, now standing, laid down a field of fire in the direction of the two ambushers hiding in the palm trees just over a hundred meters away.

"This house!" he yelled. "Take cover inside this house!" The Marines sprinted into an abandoned house on the edge of the palm grove. More SAW bursts and more M16 shots followed, and then the patrol's second ambush ceased. Draper, his squad, and the combat engineers moved on.

Minutes later, they linked up with another squad on a patrol led by Second Lieutenant Josh Booth, their platoon commander. The Haditha deployment was Booth's first experience in combat. Draper liked Booth—everyone in the platoon and in Echo as a whole liked him. A smart and diligent leader, Booth, like the other lieutenants of Echo, spent as much time outside the wire as possible. He also got to know all the Marines in his platoon, including Draper. Draper also knew of Booth's excitement over the recent birth of his daughter; his anticipation of meeting her mirrored that of Scholl, a good friend of Draper's.

Draper spoke with his lieutenant for a few minutes, then posted up next to a palm tree to act as rear security element as the other Marines, led by Booth, continued forward. Draper "took a knee," knelt on one knee and used the other to brace his SAW as he scanned the area. He heard Booth's footsteps melt into the distance as the element of Marines quietly continued their patrol.

CRACK! Draper scanned the streets. *No muzzle flash,* he thought. *Only one shot! A sniper!*

"Booth's hit!" he heard a Marine yell.

"No! No!" Draper continued to hold security as the sniper melted into the background of the city. He resisted the urge to sprint to Booth's aid. He continued to scan, to watch, his trigger finger ready. *Please be okay!* Draper thought. *We're not supposed to lose the boss, we can't lose the platoon commander. Just can't! His wife, his son, his newborn daughter—*

In Echo's COC, Second Lieutenant Ben Early heard the urgent medevac request come in over the radio. "Single shot to the head," the voice stated over the receiver. Early, a good friend of Booth, immediately put in a request for a Dustoff, then raced to lead the ground portion of the evacuation. As it was for Booth, this deployment was Early's first taste of combat. Sergeant William Davidson and Lance Corporal William Burke then took over the coordination of the Dustoff's extraction operation.

Early, sprinting to a waiting "highback" Humvee, a lightly armored version of the vehicle used to transport individual troops and wounded Marines, thought, *Single shot to the head, just like Sandvick Monroe.* As he jumped into the back of the highback, he recalled his last memory of Sandvick Monroe alive. *Strong, funny, vibrant, tireless, always happy.* Then he flashed to the image of Sandvick Monroe's bloody, lifeless body after the sniper shot. *Single shot to the head.*

The highback and two other Humvees tore out the gate of the FOB and raced down Boardwalk, then skidded to a halt minutes later. Early jumped out and sprinted toward his friend lying flat on the ground. Early took one look at Booth and knew that he wouldn't make it. The round had hit him just below the helmet, on his forehead, like the shot to Sandvick Monroe. Early and the Marines tried to save Booth, despite the wound's fatal location. The convoy skidded around street corners heading toward the LZ as the Army Dustoff roared toward the soccer field.

But Booth had died almost instantly when the sniper's round struck him. A corpsman at the LZ declared him deceased. Early and others zipped him into a body bag.

"Burke," Davidson said. "You're gonna escort Booth back to Al Asad. They're gonna need your help."

Burke, however, at the COC, didn't know Booth had died. He arrived at the LZ to see Lieutenant Early holding Booth's helmet, his face streaked with tears. Early stood next to the body bag.

Burke helped lift the body bag and carry it under the rotor wash and through the warm, pungent exhaust of the Black Hawk. The Marines slid it inside the helicopter, then Burke sat next to Booth. Early, now sobbing, handed Burke William Booth's bloodstained helmet.

This isn't real, Burke thought. *How can this be happening?* Burke cradled the platoon commander's helmet and stared at the body bag. The sound of the Hawk's engines spinning up cued Burke to look out at the Marines standing just outside the rotor wash of the helicopter. Stone-faced, they watched the Dustoff lift into the air. The FOB and LZ shrank in Burke's field of view as the helicopter raced toward Al Asad.

SERGEANT DENNIS GILBERT held one of the most difficult jobs in the battalion during the deployment. A member of the "stay-behind" element because of an injury, Dennis greeted the returning wounded and helped coordinate family notifications of the deceased. He also participated in some of the casualty notifications, when family members first learned that their loved one had died.

Weeks earlier, Gilbert had greeted Second Lieutenant Tin Nguyen, a platoon commander in Golf Company. During a firefight in Haqlaniyah, an AQI fighter shot a round that hit him in his right calf, blowing a golf-ball-sized chunk out of it. After a medevac to Al Asad, Nguyen headed to Landstuhl, then back to Hawaii. During his recuperation there, Gilbert got to know Nguyen and learned that he and Booth had gone to high school together. After high school, Nguyen and Booth each then enrolled in the Citadel, a military college in South Carolina. There, they became good friends and each was destined to become a Marine Corps infantry officer. And, coincidentally, they both landed in the same battalion as second lieutenants.

The news of Booth's passing floored Gilbert. He thought of the man's wife, his son, and his infant daughter. Then he thought of Nguyen, whom he visited daily. He saw Nguyen the day he learned the terrible news but couldn't tell the lieutenant until Booth's next of kin had been notified.

Late the next night, after Josh Booth's wife learned of her husband's passing, Gilbert walked into Nguyen's hospital room. "Sir," Gilbert said.

"Yes?" Nguyen responded.

"Lieutenant Booth died, sir. Sniper shot to the head."

Nguyen said nothing, then began sobbing uncontrollably in his hospital bed.

14

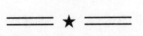

THE INTIMACY OF IT ALL

"THESE WILL HELP YOU GO TO SLEEP." A FELLOW MARINE ON THE flight home from Afghanistan had handed Lance Corporal Edwardo Lopez a couple of pills. Lopez, an infantryman with Fox Company, had taken part in a number of critical operations during 2/3's deployment to eastern Afghanistan. On his way home, unable to sleep and his knees in pain, he took the pills. A week later, Lopez "popped positive" for a controlled substance, Valium, for which he did not have a prescription. He adamantly denied knowing that the pills were Valium and, faced with a trial and separation from the Marine Corps, waived certain rights just so he could be with his Marines for their deployment to the Triad. Not wanting to let his fellow Marines down, he pled his case to Lieutenant Colonel Donnellan, who, though outside the court martial process, decided to give Lopez a second chance and let him participate on the deployment.

Deploying with Fox Company to Iraq, Lopez moved into the Barwana FOB. Despite daily attacks on the base and on all patrols outside the wire, morale remained strong throughout the company, notably with Lopez. Even with the legal problems looming over him, and the heat, enemy attacks, and wretched living conditions at the Fox Company FOB, Lopez always remained positive, motivated.

A few days after an AQI sniper killed Echo Company's Second Lieutenant Josh Booth, Lopez and his squad departed the Barwana FOB for a patrol of an area just a quarter mile distant. Lopez climbed to the roof of a building and laid down in the prone position behind his M16. The aerie provided him with a sweeping view of the neighborhood where other Marines of his squad patrolled.

CRACK! The sound of a single gunshot resonated through the area. Then silence—just one shot, no more. The Marines checked each other. No one heard a whizzing sound, which indicated a round zinging by a few feet above one's head, nor the SNAP! of a round just inches away.

"Lopez is hit!" a Marine roared. The sniper had hit him in the neck. Blood pooled beneath him. The squad's corpsman fought to stabilize Lopez as the rotors of a Dustoff Black Hawk began rotating. Lopez smiled and tried to speak. Then he turned ashen. He fought to stay alive, but by the time the Dustoff landed, he had died.

The Marines continued their patrol, now with the sole aim of identifying the sniper.

A name emerged a few days later. A human intelligence specialist attached to the company learned that years ago AQI had recruited a local boy from Barwana, taught him to be a sniper, then deployed him to Ramadi. Because of the Awakening and increased pressure on the terrorist group, this man, now twenty years old, had returned and continued to work for Al Qaeda in Iraq. He had killed a number of Marines in Ramadi but had yet to take anyone's life in Barwana—until Lopez. Armed with the address of the sniper's mother, Corporal Mark Perna, a close friend of Lopez, led his squad to hunt the man, named Bilal Maiz.

"I hate that my son has joined with Al Qaeda!" the mother cried. She was speaking through an interpreter who worked with the Marines. Perna looked at the crying mother, finding it incredibly odd that he stood in the home of a woman whose son had just killed one of his close friends.

The intimacy of it all, he thought.

"Here." She handed Perna a sack of cash—money from the Saddam era, which by this time held no value at all.

Why is she handing me all of this money? He handed it back to her, then he and his squad searched the home. They found nothing, not a trace of the sniper. The squad prepared to file out of the house, Perna leading the way.

CRACK!—CRACK!—CRACK! Three men, each holding an AK-47, jumped in front of the door and opened fire on the squad. Perna lunged backward, slamming his back to the floor, then returned fire at the men, just ten feet from him. *How am I not hit?* He and the Marines behind him squeezed off round after round at the attackers.

As quickly as they attacked, they broke contact and bolted. Perna jumped up off the floor and he and his squad rushed outside. Nothing. Gone. They had disappeared. Perna burned with frustration. He knew that one of the three men had to be the sniper—possibly all three were snipers.

The squad again spoke with the mother, but she could offer no clues. She was just Bilal Maiz's mother and had no knowledge of his activities with AQI, only that he had joined their ranks. He didn't live with her and rarely visited.

THE INCIDENT MARKED yet another in a long series of "SIG-ACTS," significant actions, by the enemy, all of which had one component in common: quick and easy egress. If the enemy couldn't get away, it wouldn't attack. As Donnellan and Mc-Cloud continued to formulate their strategy to retake the Triad for the locals, this one characteristic of each SIGACT stood out more and more as crucial. The commanders Donnellan and McCloud realized that the key lay not in keeping AQI out but in keeping it in, not allowing egress or fast escape. If an egress wasn't available, AQI would never attempt to attack in the first place.

The commanders were beginning to understand this important component of the enemy's attack plans, and they had already sent one patrol out to the palm groves with this knowledge in mind. But devising a detailed counterplan, at that point, still required more information—and an approval to put it into effect.

15

A HAVEN OF SCUM AND VILLAINY

TOWARD THE END OF OCTOBER, WHILE AQI CONTINUED TO RAMP up its operations and bring in yet more fighters, fanning and fueling the conflagration burning throughout 2/3's AO, senior battalion planners, notably Major Trane McCloud, saw a path toward victory ever more clearly. As they worked on instituting a new plan, other aspects of the counterinsurgency were beginning to bear fruit.

The battalion had always maintained a ferocious outside-the-wire presence, leaving no corner of the AO untrodden. Nor had it left any resource unused or even underused. The Marines of the battalion had worked tirelessly with elements of the Iraqi Army. The Island Warriors had built on 3/3's progress with the IA and, as a result, they were able to forge ahead with that component of the fight. They continued to train elements of the Iraqi Army on a wide spectrum of warfighting capabilities, including intelligence gathering, operations planning, and then mission execution.

Working with locals, the Marines had identified local leaders in business and politics who sought to transition the area back into firm control by the local populace. The battalion's companies had continued to work with the IP throughout the region, notably in the city of Haditha. There, more IP officers trickled into Farouk's ranks, and he and his men, in turn, provided ever-more valuable intelligence, "ground truthing," and cultural and situational awareness regarding AQI.

During this intelligence gathering, Farouk identified one location that he determined to be one of the most important, if not the most important, areas for Al Qaeda throughout the Triad: Bani Dahir, what the Marines called "Bonnie-D," a small neighborhood straddling southern Haditha and northern Haqlaniyah.

"This is where all the bad guys are," Colonel Farouk explained. "This is where they enter Haditha from, this is where they gather, where they plan, where they have meetings. If you want to stop attacks in Haditha, go there."

"It's a haven of scum and villainy," said Captain Tracy of the infamous area Bonnie-D. "We're gonna go in there and clean it out."

"THAT CAR," SAID Corporal John Hunsberger, the leader of an Echo mounted patrol traversing the southern edge of Haditha. "That black sedan. Looks suspicious. He's following our convoy." Hunsberger radioed the other vehicles in the patrol. "Let's set up a blocking position."

The convoy maneuvered throughout the streets to get behind the vehicle. Lance Corporal Travis Zabroski, in another vehicle in the convoy, popped a red "pen flare," a small pyrotechnic device used to warn vehicles to stop. The vehicle sped away.

"Don't lose it!" Hunsberger yelled to his driver. The car tore down streets and around corners—then missed a turn. WHUMP! The sedan crashed into a light pole adjacent to a metalworking shop just a block from the Euphrates, right at the northern edge of Bonnie-D.

The Marines jumped out and surrounded the vehicle. Off to the side, fifteen men stood and watched. "All fighting-age males," Zabroski observed, speaking to Lance Corporal Jacob Kareus, an Echo Marine with the patrol. The two Marines approached the trunk as other Marines helped three men out of the car, then carefully guarded them. Kareus and Zabroski opened the trunk. Inside they found stacks of US one-hundred-dollar bills, medical supplies, and shovels. "For digging IED holes," Zabroski said.

"This isn't a good situation," Kareus said, taking note of the group of men staring at the Marines. Twenty-year-old Lance Corporal Daniel Chaires stood just off to the side of Zabroski and Kareus, looking outward, watching, ready.

CRACK! Zabroski looked over to see Chaires slump to the ground. "Corpsman up!" Zabroski yelled, jumping to check Chaires. Doc Oppliger sprinted toward the downed Marine. CRACK!—CRACK!—CRACK!—CRACK!—CRACK! Volleys of automatic fire opened up from at least four positions. The group of men vanished.

Another Humvee skidded to a halt, blocking Chaires and Zabroski from enemy fire. Marines of the squad identified and engaged firing positions. Lance Corporal Travis Ledbetter, manning an M240 machine gun from the turret of the just-arrived Humvee, opened up on all positions. *BRRRRRRRRRRRR!* Enemy rounds whizzed, snapped, and pinged off all vehicles of the convoy.

"Marine down! Request QRF!" Hunsberger announced over the radio, then passed a grid. A quick reaction force convoy tore out of the Echo FOB. James Steuter, in a convoy departing the dam, heard the distress call.

Doc Oppliger rolled Chaires onto his back and opened his flak jacket. His bowels hung out. "You're gonna be okay, man!" Doc said to Chaires, who struggled to breathe. "You'll be fine. You're gonna make it!" Oppliger saw that the round had entered from the side of the flak, but he didn't see an exit wound.

Protected by two Humvees, with Ledbetter laying down fire at every enemy position, Doc Oppliger took the young Marine's flak completely off and rolled him to the side. He spotted a tiny bit of blood on his back, then rolled him back over. "You're gonna make it!" Chaires fell unconscious. "Chaires! Chaires!" Oppliger yelled. He didn't respond.

CRACK! CRACK! CRACK—CRACK! Zabroski fired round after round at the attackers, now massing in greater numbers just to the south of the Marines. "Ugh!" he yelled. CRACK—CRACK! "I just pulled my hamstring."

"You didn't pull your hamstring!" Oppliger yelled. "You just got shot!" Blood spread out along Zabroski's upper right pant leg.

CRACK—CRACK! The QRF arrived as the volume of fire exploded, from both sides.

"Welch!" Oppliger yelled to Navy Hospital Corpsman Tyler Welch. Doc Welch sprinted to Oppliger. "Keep an eye on Chaires while I patch up Zabroski!" CRACK! CRACK! CRACK! CRACK! Zabroski continued to put rounds down range as the blood continued to pour out of his wound. Doc Oppliger pulled out his shears and crawled over to Zabroski.

"What!"

"I gotta patch you up!" CRACK! CRACK! Zabroski swapped out magazines. CRACK! CRACK! Oppliger cut into Zabroski's pants.

FSEEEEEEW—BOOM! FSEEEEEEW—BOOM! FSEEE-EEEW—BOOM!

"RPGs!" A volley of rocket-propelled grenades sailed into the Marines' position, exploding all around them as they impacted buildings, trees, and power poles. Power lines careened down from the explosions.

"Second Marine down!" Steuter heard over his radio.

"We gotta get down there!" Steuter's convoy approached a notorious IED site.

"Chaires is in real bad shape!" Steuter's radio blared.

"GRENADE!" Kareus yelled. He saw a hand grenade fly over a wall and land near Hunsberger. "GRENADE!" Hunsberger dove onto the ground. BOOM!

"Ugh!" Shrapnel tore into Hunsberger's right calf. He rolled away from the explosion, then jumped up and "pogo-sticked" over to Kareus, hopping on one leg. *FSEEEEEW*—BOOM! *FSEEEEEW*—BOOM! *FSEEEEEW*—BOOM! More RPGs erupted all around them.

"We have three Marines down!" Steuter heard.

"Ahhhh!" Kareus gulped as a round tore into his left calf.

"Four Marines down!"

BRRRR! Ledbetter continued to lay down streams of fire as the other Marines took well-placed head and body shots. Three, four, five enemy fighters fell. One guy appeared to evaporate as a hail of Ledbetter's rounds tore into him. Six, seven, eight enemy down.

"Let's get out of here!" Oppliger yelled as he loaded Chaires into a Humvee. A Dustoff streaked low over the desert en route to the soccer field LZ. Kareus and Hunsberger limped over to the Humvee with Chaires. *BRRRR!* Ledbetter continued to lay down fire. *FSEEEEEW*—BOOM! *FSEEEEEW*—BOOM! *FSEEEEEW*—BOOM! Another hail of RPGs exploded around the Marines. "ZABROSKI!" Oppliger yelled. "LET'S GO! YOU'RE SHOT!"

"I'm fine!" CRACK! CRACK! CRACK! CRACK! "Go without me! I'm fine!" Oppliger jumped in the Humvee with Chaires, Hunsberger, Kareus, and Doc Welch.

"Let's go! Oppliger roared. The driver of the Humvee tore down Boardwalk to the soccer field LZ.

"Let's go, let's get down there. Those guys are in it," Steuter said. His convoy was stopped at a bridge over a wadi that had recently sustained damage from a massive IED—it fortunately didn't cause any serious injuries or deaths, just some minor damage to a seven-ton, but it had made the bridge unusable. Steuter's seven-ton went first, driving down into the wadi, and then back up the other side. Then the second vehicle, a Humvee, passed through. The third in the line, another Humvee, descended into the dry river bed. The driver, a Navy Seabee attached to the battalion to undertake some construction projects at various FOBs in the AO, kept the vehicle moving smoothly along in the tracks of Steuter's seven-ton.

Three hundred meters in the distance, atop a small rise with a perfect view of the convoy, an AQI operative touched two wires to a six-volt battery. *WHUMP!* A massive explosion erupted. Bloodied underwear landed on the right-side rearview mirror of Steuter's seven-ton. The Marines jumped out to see the smoking wreckage of the Humvee. "Sweep for secondaries!" Steuter yelled. "There could be more explosives!" Blood and body parts littered the area around the destroyed truck. The IED instantly killed the driver, Navy Construction Electrician 2nd Class Charles Komppa. The tremendous explosion knocked everyone in the fourth vehicle, also a Humvee, temporarily unconscious.

"Let's get out and help find survivors!" Sergeant Jason Tarr, the commander of the fourth Humvee, said when he regained consciousness. Steuter ran up to a Marine lying facedown near the wreckage. One of his legs had been blown off. He rolled the Marine onto his back. "Brown," Steuter said.

Nineteen-year-old Donald Brown, an Echo Marine, had been in the turret of the Humvee. The explosion killed him instantly. *BRRRR!* The sound of an AQI machine gun tore through the area. Bullets whizzed overhead. *BRRRR!* Another salvo erupted. Rounds impacted the bloody area the Marines searched. Then the ambush ended.

One person remained to be found, Navy Hospital Corpsman Larry Perry. "Here he is!" Steuter located him a hundred meters away, amid a swath of blood and body parts, pinned under one of the Humvee's doors. Steuter threw the heavy door off to the side. Perry was holding onto life, barely. Another urgent medevac call went out. Another Dustoff spun up at Al Asad. More lives back home changed forever.

CRACK!—CRACK! CRACK!—CRACK! Zabroski continued firing at the AQI fighters coming at the Marines. Another Humvee pulled up next to him. In the turret, Lance Corporal Timothy Brown readied his Mk32 six-shot semiautomatic 40mm grenade launcher. To their left, a fighter tried to flank the Marines. Brown saw him and took aim just as the fighter leveled his AK-47 at Zabroski. THUMP!—THUMP!—THUMP!—THUMP! Brown unleashed a torrent of the high-explosive rounds. The fighter disintegrated.

Lance Corporal Jared Campbell, also with Timothy Brown, spotted another fighter emerging, trying to outflank them. The man aimed his AK-47 at Brown. CRACK! CRACK! Campbell fired two rounds, striking the man in the shoulder. THUMP!—THUMP! Brown fired the Mk32 again, striking the fighter. A cloud of pink mist hung in the air, punctuated by the AK-47—and an arm—spinning above it.

BRRRR! Ledbetter unleashed yet another volley from his 240. The enemy fire stopped. Over the radio, Campbell heard Captain Tracy call in two Abrams tanks and two helicopter gunships. "We're going to obliterate these guys!" Already, twelve AQI lay dead in the streets. Zabroski, preparing to go back to the FOB, scanned the distance for more. A Dustoff, bound for the soccer field LZ, screamed overhead.

Marines and Army medics loaded Chaires, Hunsberger, and Kareus onto the Hawk. The medics went straight to work on Chaires as the turboshaft engines screamed and the helicopter's rotors bit into the air, lifting the bird off the ground.

Chaires lapsed in and out of consciousness as the medics fought for his life. As Zabroski passed through the gate, Zack Drill ran up to him. "You got to get on the medevac bird!"

"What?" Zabroski asked.

"They're turning around to get you," Drill yelled. "Come on, I'll drive you to the LZ!" Drill's Humvee skidded into the soccer field just as the Dustoff roared overhead, then touched down. Zabroski, without pants, hobbled onto the Hawk.

"Chaires!" Zabroski yelled as the Dustoff lifted into the sky. His wounded friend blinked at him. Chaires held on, barely. The medics could do no more; he needed surgery, and that might not even save him. He had sustained massive internal injuries to a number of organs. "Chaires!" Zabroski yelled again. "You're gonna make it!" Chaires smiled. Zabroski talked to him about his home, his family, the beach near their base in Hawaii.

Nineteen-year-old Lance Corporal Daniel Chaires took his last breath less than two minutes later. The other wounded Marines, adrenaline fading from their veins, sat stone-faced for the remainder of the journey.

16

═══ ★ ═══

A BREEZE OF CHANGE

A NUMBER OF UNITS FROM OUTSIDE THE BATTALION SUPPORTED the campaign that 2/3 waged in the Triad over the course of 2/3's deployment. These included outside Marine Corps units that temporarily attached to the battalion via their higher headquarters. In late October 2006, a scout sniper team from the 1st Battalion of the 8th Marine Regiment arrived and integrated with scout sniper operations in the city of Haditha—specifically, counter-sniper operations, where the hunters become the hunted.

At the time, 1/8 had been the GCE, or ground combat element, of the 24th Marine Expeditionary Unit. Similarly, although not under the command of 2/3, the 2nd Battalion of the 4th Marine Regiment joined the fight for the Anbar Province in the fall of 2006. 2/4, the ground combat element for the 15th Marine Expeditionary Unit, established "Camp Bastard" as a "battalion landing team" on the far outskirts of Barwana for Regimental Combat Team 7. 2/4's operations and personnel would complement those of 2/3 over the course of a number of months—and 2/3's would likewise complement theirs.

"We're gonna do something that's never been done before," Captain Tracy proclaimed to his Marines during a late October briefing. "We're gonna bring Halloween to Haditha." Those before him laughed. "It isn't funny!" he said. "But Operation Halloween in Haditha is Halloween in reverse. We'll be going door to door like we do back home, but instead of asking for candy, we'll be giving it out to the kids and asking what their parents need," he said. "So start digging through the trash and come up with costumes. And all those care packages from home—with candy and beef jerky, dump all of them into one big pot."

"I don't think we're gonna get approval on this, sir," Lieutenant Ben Early said.

"We're not going to ask for approval, lieutenant," Tracy responded. "We're just going to go out and do it. It's going to be [part of our] COIN, but also an information operation," he said. "We're going to hand out flyers introducing us, letting the locals know that we're here for them."

"But what happens if we take contact, if there are casualties?" Early asked. "How are we going to explain showing up in Al Asad in Halloween costumes? You'll get relieved."

Crowe already wants to relieve me, Tracy thought to himself. "But we didn't come out here to worry about Crowe."

Information operations, or IOs, rank as one of the most effective actions to implement in a counterinsurgency campaign. They're also some of the most difficult to undertake for nonlocal forces because of language and cultural barriers. A sentence on a flyer in perfect "textbook Arabic" may, in reality, relay an insult or just strike locals as comically awkward.

Furthermore, as Tracy explained to his Marines, "AQI doesn't need to wait for approval. They just do their own IO." Al Qaeda spread its words through mosque loudspeakers, over radio, through phone calls, flyers, graffiti, and in person (including hanging corpses). A statement as simple as "we'll be here after the Marines leave" was a powerful, long-resonating salvo in their IO campaign.

IO "missions" fall into essentially two categories: long-term, overarching message campaigns, and those triggered by an incident such as an IED blast that wounds a local. Whereas AQI could immediately point the finger at the Americans, the Marines needed to have a message they wanted to send out approved—and approval took upward of a week and the message was often sanitized to such an extent as to be meaningless.

"The locals will never forget this IO campaign," Tracy said, smiling. In addition to patrolling, standing post, dodging mortars at the Haditha FOB, and cleaning burn shitters, Echo Marines scavenged for every last piece of candy they could find. They also scrounged for materials to craft costumes. Tracy involved Farouk, who helped the Marines with the geography of Operation Halloween. Tracy wanted to learn not only which neighborhoods might be most receptive to the dressed-up Marines, but which ones had children who would appreciate the gifts the most, that is, the poorest areas.

"How are we going to come up with flyers, then?" Early asked. In addition to approving IO, Marine Corps higher headquarters also produced materials for the battalion to use. But the battalion would be on its own this time.

"You know what a ditto machine is, lieutenant?" Tracy asked.

"I vaguely do, sir," Early responded.

"You ever seen one, or smell one?" he asked. "They have that roller, and the blue ink. Makes that rhythmic sound as it churns out dittos for classroom use." Early stared at the company commander and shook his head.

"My parents mentioned them a couple times," the lieutenant said.

"Schools used them before Xerox copy machines got cheap enough for schools to buy," Tracy said. "And they have one right here, or Billy Parker over in Civil Affairs has one. He found one, and boxes of paper and ink, in an abandoned school here."

"You know how to use it?" Early asked.

"I do," Tracy said. "I was that guy in second grade who knew how to fix the projector—and set up the ditto machine."

Working with Marwan, one of Echo's interpreters, the company commander drafted a single-sheet flyer introducing the town to "reverse Halloween." It also stated their intention: to stand up for the local population, to bring back peace.

"Well look at that," Tracy said on October 31, just before passing outside the wire to begin Operation Halloween in Haditha. "We all have the same costume," he said, looking at all the Marines headed out on patrol with him. "What do we call this costume?" The question brought laughter. "I think it's Robocop meets the Staten Island Dump." The Marines had cobbled together scraps of plastic, crushed cans, and MRE boxes to fashion crude robot costumes—that, they hoped, wouldn't impede their movement, especially if ambushed.

"This really isn't the best idea, sir," Early said. "If something happens, and a lot can go wrong—"

Tracy stared at the lieutenant.

"It's more than worth it," the captain said. "Trust me."

Each Marine carried a bag stuffed with candy, muffins, beef jerky, Slim Jims, summer sausage, and even some MRE leftovers. "Don't be handing out MREs," Tracy said jokingly. "We want the people to like us, not hate us." The captain handed out stacks of flyers, but not before holding one up to his nose. He took a deep sniff and exclaimed, "Smells like the second grade!"

For hours, squads of Echo Company Marines fanned out in Haditha, knocking on doors and handing out candy and flyers. Hours later, all returned. The enemy didn't fire a single shot during the entire operation.

Not only did they get their message out, the Echo Marines also gained that much more traction with the local population. Their absurd costumes brought laughter from children and even smiles from some adults, and the hundreds of pounds of gifts proved intent in a way no flyer ever could convey.

The operation also boosted morale, keeping thoughts of death and injury and of those lost away for a brief time. In retrospect, Operation Halloween in Haditha marked the first breeze of change in the storm of adversity in which 2/3 dwelled.

"And now that we just proved the success of the concept," Tracy announced, "we need to start planning for Operation Christmas in Haditha. So, get all your family and friends to send us presents not for us, but for the local children. And we need some Santa and Elves costumes."

By ten o'clock that night, all Marines of Operation Halloween in Haditha passed back inside the wire unscathed. But only a few hours later, in the early morning of the first of November, AQI would strike again and bring more tragedy.

"AIR'S GOING RED," Captain Tracy said as the message came through on "mIRC," a secure form of internet relay chat, one of the many forms of communication that connected the various components of the battalion. "Red Air" indicated that air assets, including Dustoff medevac helicopters, could not fly because of dangerous atmospheric conditions. In Al Anbar Province, a Red Air call usually came only with dust storms or sandstorms. For ground personnel, the call always sparked a heightened sense of seriousness—if AQI struck and inflicted injuries, regardless of the severity, a medevac couldn't launch until conditions improved. Poor conditions could cause a crash and yet more injuries or deaths. Red Air sometimes lasted just a half hour, but could last an entire day. As such, if "air was going red," then patrols would either "go firm," meaning stop and take up a defensive position in a well-covered location, or RTB (return to base), if time and distance allowed.

Shortly after the close of Operation Halloween in Haditha, a team of 1/8 scout snipers squeezed through the Mouse Hole to begin a counter-sniper operation in the city. Though the air

hadn't gone red yet, conditions outside continued to deterio-
rate. Like other scout sniper operations, the team had recon-
noitered a hide earlier while on patrol with Echo Marines. As
the air conditions approached red status, the 1/8 snipers neared
their hide. When the "air is red" message arrived, fine dust had
already enveloped Haditha, blotting out the stars, distant light,
even streetlights.

BOOM! A massive explosion erupted. James Steuter was
monitoring a number of radio nets while on QRF duty. "It's
close," he said. "Really close, like right outside the FOB." Steuter ran through the possibilities—and immediately figured that
the explosion most likely involved the sniper team because of
the time of their departure and the proximity of the blast.

The scout snipers called the COC seconds later. One of their
team, Corporal Gary Koehler, had stepped on an IED, instantly
killing him. The blast gravely wounded another. "What's your
pos?" Steuter asked, needing their position to move to them.

"We don't know," the team responded. "Down near the
river." A QRF convoy sped out the FOB's gate. By that time in
the deployment, Steuter and other Echo Marines had traversed
so much of the city that they didn't need maps. He knew that
the team might be on a street too narrow for the convoy to
quickly move through. He and others of the QRF jumped out
of their vehicles and sprinted toward the river. He heard yelling, then vectored onto their position. He called in an urgent
medevac—but air conditions remained at red status. With one
dead, Steuter and a corpsman inspected the injured.

"This is bad," the corpsman said. The explosion had peppered one of the Marines with chunks of shrapnel and had
sliced into one of his eyes. Steuter called in more details about
the condition of the injured.

At Al Asad, a Dustoff crew made a decision—regardless of
conditions, they'd make a go to save the Marine's life. The Black
Hawk tore through the dust storm. Steuter and others loaded
the injured Marine into the back of a highback Humvee. The

road from the location of the IED to the soccer field LZ, how-ever, would likely be laced with IEDs because it was a dirt track and near the FOB.

"I'll drive him," Steuter said. "I'll get him through it." As he drove, every muscle in his body clenched, waiting for a blast to envelop his Humvee. Steuter maneuvered down the dirt road and then into the soccer field. Minutes later, the Dustoff roared overhead, picked up the wounded man, then returned to Al Asad, where surgeons saved the injured Marine's life.

17

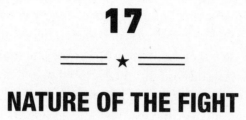

NATURE OF THE FIGHT

In the Haditha Triad, the battalion's campaign, like all successful COIN campaigns, required taking a conceptual idea and making it real in particular circumstances. The "end state" of a successful COIN campaign was painted with the broadest stroke of the conceptual brush: a restored security situation, a renewed government, and a flourishing economy for the population.

For 2/3, getting to that goal in the particular circumstances of their AO meant they had to identify a number of interrelated goals (stand up a police force, rid the area of AQI, find a mayor and city council, etc.), outline synergizing efforts to achieve these interrelated goals, and then identify the specific people to undertake each of the myriad efforts. Now with people in place throughout the AO, and with individual operations ongoing across the battlespace, the battalion staff formulated a final plan of efforts in early November.

The key to overall success, Major Trane McCloud knew, was enduring security. And the initial operational mechanism to achieve that, he saw, was to control who enters and who exits the Triad. Troves of after-action reports and intelligence data showed that egress was the primary consideration for all AQI operations in the Triad. Al Qaeda knew it couldn't win a pitched battle with Marines, so in order to fight and then live to fight another day, they needed escape routes, first and foremost. Therefore, McCloud sought operational ways to deny them these escape routes. Once Al Qaeda was defeated, he calculated, then the area could finish reestablishing endemic security forces and rebuild the local government and economy.

To control who came and went, Marine battalions had long-established entry control points and vehicle control points throughout the area. However, AQI simply avoided these and came and went through the desert or by way of the river. The Marines and IP had interdicted a number of these infiltrators during patrols and operations, but even with all Marines, IP, and Iraqi Army members available—patrolling nonstop and without rest—Al Qaeda still found a porous section into which it could slip and then escape.

McCloud studied everything he could, both in the Triad and throughout Iraq. After poring over maps, spreadsheets, and reports, he devised his plan. It consisted of three *B* elements: berm, BATS, badge. They'd use Marine Combat Engineers to construct a berm, essentially a dirt wall, around the Triad. Simultaneously, they'd step up their use of the BATS, or the Biometrics Automated Toolset System. The BATS consisted of a digital scanner, a fingerprint reader, an iris scanner, and a Toughbook computer. The system allowed them to build a database of individuals based on their biometric data and biographical data—address, family and tribal ties, law enforcement data, and any other information that might tie an individual to a terrorist or insurgent organization. The third *B*, badging, would provide access badges for both individuals and vehicles. A tiered system of badges could control who came and went, and which vehicles came and went in the Triad.

McCloud and Donnellan had discussed the berming idea since before ever stepping foot in the Triad. Berms had been constructed before in Iraq, and they had proved successful, but none had ever been built on such a large scale. Walling off an entire urban region would require an enormous effort. But, they figured, they could get the resources if the plan was approved by their higher command.

Of course, the Marines couldn't berm the Euphrates. They could, however, establish presence on some of the islands in the Euphrates that AQI used. Norm Cooling and 3/3 had identified the islands as possible locations of insurgent activity, although operations proved difficult to conduct on them because of logistical difficulties. McCloud and Donnellan saw control of the Euphrates as critical to complementing a berm. They decided it could be done by patrolling with the "gunboats" of the DSU, or Dam Support Unit, attached to 2/3 and, most importantly, by reaching out to the inhabitants of the islands using classic COIN tactics.

The entire plan would require approval, which meant dealing with Colonel Crowe, who Donnellan and others felt was increasingly hostile to 2/3, Captain Matt Tracy in particular. Meanwhile, enemy activity continued to flare throughout the Triad in early November. The Marines, with their partners of the IP and Iraqi Army, however, fought back, always with their long-term mission in mind.

THE DEATHS OF Echo Marine Lance Corporal Donald Brown and Navy Seabee Charles Komppa had increased AQI focus on the location of the explosion that killed them. Whereas it was a horrific tragedy for the Marines and the family members and friends of the fallen, it represented a tremendous success for Al Qaeda, which wanted to repeat its victory that caused so much agony.

With the bridge out, convoys needed to descend into the dry wash to move between the dam and other locations in the AO. With a bridge, AQI had just a narrow passageway on which to hide IEDs. With the passageway across that section of the AO widened, Al Qaeda had that much more real estate in which to hide primary IEDs, and even secondary ones, and possibly tertiary explosives. Furthermore, because of its remoteness in the open desert, AQI could come and go much more freely than in other parts of the area of operations.

By the fall of 2006, AQI had perfected creating and emplacing IEDs. The AQI fighters made a science of their deadly craft, using a wide range of documentation, field manuals, and even instructional videos. The purpose was always the same: terrorize and force a group to comply with them by killing and maiming. The process started with identifying the type of target—unshielded people or, more commonly, people protected in vehicles.

Killing and maiming people inside a vehicle requires a much more powerful explosion than ending the life of a pedestrian. AQI sourced the explosives for IEDs typically from old munitions like mortar rounds, artillery rounds, or antiaircraft rounds. Sometimes they got their hands on actual land mines, either antitank mines or antipersonnel mines, like the one that killed Corporal Gary Koehler, the scout sniper from 1/8. Sometimes AQI procured raw explosives, like C-4 or Semtex. Sometimes they used dynamite. In Iraq, AQI "enhanced" some of their IEDs with tanks of propane, which acted as a booster of explosive yield and an incendiary agent. Another type of IED, an EFP, or explosively formed penetrator, saw some use in Iraq, but not in 2/3's area of operations. EFPs, which form a metal projectile through the kinetic energy of an explosion, can punch through heavy armor but require precision machining and specialized metal components.

With an explosive in their hands, the terrorists then added an initiator, the device that makes an explosive explode. AQI often used electrically activated commercial blasting caps. Rarely, they crafted their own initiators with electronics and small amounts of explosives. The triggering mechanism, the device that activates the initiator, followed in the manufacturing process. AQI used pressure-plate triggers and tripwires for IEDs that victims activated, and hardwire and wireless triggers for IEDs that an on-site fighter fired. AQI delivered IEDs either statically, such as by burying them in a road, placing them in the side of a wall, or hiding them in a car, or dynamically, when an attacker would maneuver close to victims wearing a suicide vest or in a rigged vehicle. Static emplacement ranked, by far, as the most common IED delivery method AQI used in 2/3's AO. Most of these IEDs were massive, meant to obliterate vehicles and kill and maim anyone inside or near the explosion.

At a selected location, AQI typically placed static IEDs in two or three stages. First, the terrorists would have someone dig a hole. Then, typically using a vehicle, they'd have a small team place the IED, its triggering mechanism, and battery power source in the hole and bury it. If the device was victim initiated, they'd just wait for a person or vehicle to trigger the explosion. If the device was user activated, they'd send out a trigger person (and often a videographer to record the carnage) as a final stage in their process of terror.

The Marines, well aware of Al Qaeda's IED emplacement tactics, continued to refine their own counter-IED actions. They requested aviation assets such as Marine Corps AV-8B Harrier II attack jets and F/A-18D Hornets based at Al Asad to "scan" from tens of thousands of feet aloft areas that AQI repeatedly used to emplace IEDs. Using targeting pods, devices with electro-optical daylight and thermal infrared scanners, the jet operators could zoom in and identify suspicious behavior, like someone digging a hole in a road and then leaving. Once a grid was passed to a ground unit, a sniper team or a squad of Marines could set up an observation post near the hole and then wait for stage two of the emplacement process—and interdict it with well-placed shots. Sometimes helicopter gunships or attack jets took care of interdicting stage two, to the delight of the pilots.

Marines also surveilled known IED sites from the ground. After the deaths of Brown and Komppa, Lieutenant Ben Early and Marines of his platoon made interdicting AQI's emplacement of IEDs in the wadi one of their pet projects.

"You gotta want it," Captain Tracy told him. "You gotta want to get these guys trying to get us more than they want to get us. I mean, cover yourself in mud and breathe out of a reed in the Euphrates to get close enough—do whatever you gotta do." Early and his Marines began making forays at night to overwatch the patch of ground. "No matter what you do, though," Tracy always reminded his Marines before every operation, "put the people first. Don't ever put them in danger. Put yourselves in danger before you put them in danger."

THE LIEUTENANT AND a squad of his platoon's Marines departed the Echo FOB late in the night on November 3 for an "ambush patrol." A small convoy carried them north out of the Haditha FOB, then stopped about three miles from the wadi. Previously, Early and some of his Marines had identified an ideal position from which to overwatch the site, a small group of homes next to an old cemetery about three hundred meters to the south of the wadi.

"Whoa!" Early said, lunging forward. He'd tripped as he passed the small cemetery. Backing up, he inspected the ground where he tripped. He had been walking just off the side of the road on the margin of some gravestones. Before him lay two wires. "Look," he said to Corporal Leonel Cuellar, one of the Marines of his squad. "These two wires, they lead into the distance, directly toward the wadi." Cuellar scanned the distance.

"It's IED command wire," Cuellar said, "ready to be hooked onto a battery to detonate it. This is probably where they set off the device that killed Brown and the Seabee."

"Yeah," Early responded. "And there's another one ready, tied to these wires." Early called EOD and explained the situation. The IED would be reduced within an hour. In the meantime, the Marines would watch over the wadi—and the cemetery where Early stumbled on the command wire.

"Over there, sir," Cuellar said, pointing to a house adjacent to the cemetery. That's our overwatch point." The squad approached the home. Early knocked and a man opened the door. Cigarette smoke poured into the night. The lieutenant apologized in broken Arabic, then asked the man to allow the squad into the home for a few hours. He agreed.

The Marines filed inside. A group of men sat in one room, each smoking. In an adjoining room, four women sat, one noticeably pregnant. The Marines quietly walked into the empty third room of the home. Its one window faced the spot where Early found the wires tied around the rock.

"Look, sir," Cuellar said. "A light." A glimmer bobbed in the distance. The Marines focused on it, and it grew brighter.

"Uhhhhhh!" A woman's voice bellowed through the home.

"Cuellar," Early said, "check it out." The light split into two.

"Headlights," Early said. "A car coming our way."

"Ahhhhhhh!" The woman moaned louder.

"Sir," Cuellar said, walking back into the room of Marines, "that pregnant woman is about to lose some weight—she's giving birth."

The car stopped next to the command wire. Three men emerged. The woman's screams of childbirth grew louder. The Marines closely eyed the trio from the shadows. One of the men knelt next to the rock with wires tied around it. Another sat on the ground and fixed a video camera to a tripod, aiming it at the wadi. The third stood and watched from behind the two.

"Sir," Cuellar said.

"I know, Corporal," the lieutenant responded. The crying of a newborn baby rang throughout the home. "We can't engage them from here. That'll put all these people in the house in danger when they shoot back." Early paused. "We have to get behind them."

Cuellar and half the squad slipped out of the home and moved silently into the night. Early and the other Marines followed, then positioned themselves beside Cuellar. As Early approached, the man standing behind the two on the ground lunged toward the car. He pulled out an AK-47 and aimed it at Early. CRACK!—CRACK! Cuellar sent one round into his head and another into his neck. He crumpled to the ground, dead before his body flopped to a standstill. The man adjusting the video camera sprinted into the cemetery. The other leapt up and lunged toward the car. CRACK! Cuellar loosed another round. The man spun around and smacked the ground. Blood dumped onto the sand around him.

An element of Marines raced after the runner. The remainder approached the two downed AQI operatives and their vehicle. In the trunk, they found shovels and two IEDs, ready to be placed.

Cuellar stood over the bleeding man. Early joined Cuellar, standing over the dying AQI operative, very likely the one who triggered the explosive days earlier that killed Brown and Komppa. Both Cuellar and Early felt their weapons rising as if magnetically attracted to the man's head. Cuellar's straight trigger finger quivered. He felt his chest rising and falling inside his flak jacket. He thought of Brown, of all the other fallen Echo Marines of the deployment.

"We gotta call this in," Early said.

Cuellar stared silently at Early for a few seconds. "Right," the corporal said.

Captain Tracy responded to Early over the radio: "At this point he's a wounded noncombatant. I'll spin up an urgent Dustoff for him." The company commander paused. "Get him ready. Have two Marines accompany him to Al Asad."

"Roger, sir," the lieutenant responded. "Oh, there's one more medical issue going on here—"

"Yeah?"

Early explained the situation in the house. Then, "Let's get him ready for evac," Early said to Cuellar as the Marines who chased after the third man reappeared, empty-handed.

At the Echo COC, Captain Tracy ended the conversation with Early, and then said, "Nature of the fight." He slapped his hand on the desk next to the radios. "Nature of the fight."

An hour later, a Dustoff touched down near the cemetery. Medics cut the clothes off the AQI trigger man and inspected him for any hidden weapons or explosives, then loaded him onto the bird. They worked to stabilize him and prep him for surgery, just as they'd do with any other patient, friend or foe. *Nature of the fight.*

"Where's this newborn and the mother?" one of the medics asked over the *THWACK—THWACK—THWACK* of the Hawk's rotor blades and the wailing howl of its idling engines.

"This way!" As the Al Qaeda trigger man inched closer to death by the second, the medics stormed into the home. They knelt next to the mother holding her newborn. A broken-English–broken-Arabic back-and-forth ensued. She seemed fine. The baby seemed fine. The medics left her with some painkillers, then sprinted toward the Dustoff.

Early sent two of the squad's Marines with the medics, as instructed by Tracy. "Stay with the guy!" the lieutenant said. "He's your responsibility." The pilot on the sticks of the Hawk edged the collective up, and the aircraft roared into the night, disappearing from earshot less than a half minute later.

"Now we wait for EOD," Early said.

Hours later, the IED, similar to the one that had killed Brown and Komppa days earlier, exploded in the wadi. BOOM! Detonated not by an Al Qaeda trigger man but by Marine Corps explosive ordnance disposal technicians. The explosion marked one less threat to lives and limbs in the AO.

The wounded AQI operative lived. The same surgeons at Al Asad who saved Doc Perry, horrifically wounded by the IED that killed Brown and Komppa, saved him.

Nature of the fight.

18

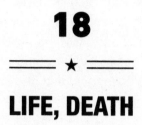

LIFE, DEATH

"I'm a dad!" roared Gunnery Sergeant Terry Elliott at the Echo FOB. Elliott's wife, Loretta, had given birth on November 10 to a baby boy. "What a day to have your firstborn," Elliott said. "The 231st Marine Corps birthday." Elliott, thirty-four, and his wife met in high school in the small town of Middleton, Tennessee, in the southwest corner of the state. He and Loretta planned for years to start a family, and they both looked forward to life after his Iraq deployment, his last. Like Mike Scholl, he spoke of his newborn, Preston, daily. "Born on the Marine Corps birthday!"

Gunny Elliott, a platoon sergeant in Whiskey Company, had come to Haditha with his platoon to reinforce Echo. With so many lost to death and injury by that point in the deployment, the battalion pulled Elliott's platoon, commanded by Second Lieutenant Brian Park, to reinforce them during a particularly high-op-tempo period. Led by intelligence from Farouk and his IP, Echo had been conducting "clearing" operations throughout the city. Each night, the operations took them to a series of houses of suspected AQI operatives and sympathizers, where they would conduct sweeps for weapons, IED-making materials, and propaganda. The netted individuals and their computer files and notebooks would then generate yet more intelligence, used for the next night's raids. Echo prevailed in Haditha—but the cornered, wounded animal remained not only capable but also ever more ferocious as Echo gained ground in the fight.

CRACK! CRACK! Rounds sailed into the Echo FOB as Mike Scholl and others prepared for a patrol on the morning of November 14. James Steuter sprinted along a wall toward Scholl. CRACK! CRACK! CRACK! Scholl dove into the turret of his Humvee as enemy tracer rounds cast bright red streaks through the air. PING! PING! PING! Rounds slammed into the truck's armor. *FSEEEEEEW*—BOOM! An RPG impacted the concrete above Steuter, sending a chunk onto his helmeted head. "Scholl!" Steuter yelled. "You got eyes-on?" *KER-CHUNK!* Scholl racked the bolt of his M240B machine gun and spun the turret around, aiming toward the origin of the fire.

"Negative!" he responded. "Can't see a single one of them!"

The ambush ended after just a few seconds. Scholl, Steuter, and others, their weapons ready, continued to scan. The attackers had fled.

Scholl returned to prepping his 240, his M16, and his other gear. Steuter prepared to head out in his seven-ton, the lead vehicle for mounted patrol. Sergeant William Davidson's squad, which included Mario Anes and William Burke, would ride in the back of Steuter's truck. Captain Tracy would accompany Davidson's squad—Farouk and his IPs had handed the company commander some compelling intelligence about an enemy cell based south of Haditha. Located in an abandoned oil-pumping facility called "K3," the cell, Farouk explained, had been responsible for a number of ambushes and IEDs. Although not part of the Echo area of operations, Tracy and his Marines would nevertheless undertake the raid, as Farouk provided the intel.

Tracy planned on visiting more than just the K3 location, however. The company commander never would forgo a chance to visit the "haven of scum and villainy," Bonnie-D, even though it was not along the most direct route to the oil-pumping station. The plan was for the patrol first to sweep through Bonnie-D, then to continue on to K3—and then possibly to visit the neighborhood again on the return.

With all the Marines of the patrol loaded, Steuter's vic rumbled out of the gate followed by three Humvees. The rear Humvee, driven by Lance Corporal Tim "Brickhead" Brown, carried Scholl in the turret, Gunnery Sergeant Marcus Wilson in the rear, and Lance Corporal Mario "Gonzo" Gonzalez in the vehicle commander's seat. A close friend to Scholl, Gonzo had served with Scholl, James Steuter, Mario Anes, and William Davidson in Echo Company during 2/3's Afghan deployment.

Here we go, Steuter said to himself as the convoy approached Bonnie-D and he saw people clear off the roadway. A man wielding a machine gun leapt from a shadowed alleyway as the convoy passed. CRACK!—CRACK!—CRACK!—CRACK! He opened up on the fourth vic. Scholl aimed his 240 and squeezed the trigger. *BRRRR!* The lance corporal sent a volley of rounds toward the attacker, who dove back into the alleyway.

"We're gettin' out," Captain Tracy said. "We're dismounting now and sweeping this whole area." The lead seven-ton, carrying Tracy and Davidson's squad, parked on a patch of road fifty meters from the Euphrates in the heart of Bonnie-D, near where AQI had just weeks earlier shot Chaires, Zabroski, Kareus, and Hunsberger. Minutes later, as Captain Tracy and Davidson's squad swept along the palm grove, Steuter had his seven-ton switch positions with Gonzo's so that the squad and Tracy could mount back up more quickly. Lance Corporal Brown parked the Humvee. Scholl scanned the distance from the truck's turret. Steuter watched closely as Mario Anes and William Burke approached his seven-ton.

Sixty meters, fifty meters, forty meters. A man walking past the truck grabbed Steuter's attention. The man pulled the pin on a hand grenade and lobbed it toward Anes and Burke. "Grenade!" Steuter yelled. The attacker darted into an alley and Steuter leapt from the seven-ton. Anes and Burke dove to the side of the street. BOOM! Steuter sprinted after the man, but he disappeared into the maze of the neighborhood.

"You getting in with us, sir?" Gunny Wilson asked Captain Tracy as he walked past the parked Humvee with Scholl manning the turret.

"No," Tracy responded. "I'm going to keep walking, keep sweeping till I get up to Corporal Steuter's seven-ton."

Steuter walked back to his truck. After the brief spray of machine gun fire and the lobbed hand grenade, all seemed still in Bonnie-D. The Marines readied to mount up again and head toward K3. Scholl continued to scan, to search.

Across the river, concealed by a small grove of palm trees, an AQI operative slid a rock to the side, revealing a six-volt battery and two thin wires. He attached one wire to one terminal, then touched the second wire to the other as he eyed the Humvee carrying Wilson, Brown, Gonzo, and Scholl.

BOOM! The explosion knocked Anes and Burke to the ground. Captain Tracy, just fifty feet from the explosion, saw only white and felt only force—force smashing him to the ground. The company commander heard nothing. Steuter sprinted toward the site of the explosion—an IED had detonated directly under the Humvee. *I was parked there just minutes ago!* he thought. The explosion obliterated the front half of the vehicle and launched the rear half high into the air. It flipped end over end, then came crashing down on the crater, upside down.

Tracy began to hear noise as he lifted himself off the ground. White dust filled the air. He could see nothing—then a telephone pole emerged from the strange haze. *Telephone pole?* He thought. *They're launching telephone poles at us now?* Whack!

The telephone pole landed just feet in front of him. "The Humvee!" he yelled as the air cleared further. The company commander spun around, looking for any visual cue. He struggled to balance himself as Steuter lunged through the clearing dust and locked eyes on Gunny Wilson, hanging upside down by a seat belt.

"I'm sorry, corporal," Wilson said to Steuter. "I'm sorry. I'm so, so sorry!" The gunnery sergeant's lower left leg hung by a thin strip of skin. Blood poured into the crater left by the blast. "I'm sorry."

Anes and Burke followed Steuter, sprinting to the destruction. Brown and Burke had become best friends during their time in 2/3 together. Anes knew what to expect as he approached the scene of devastation. He turned to Burke. "Don't come any closer to the Humvee, Burke!" Anes yelled. He didn't want Burke to see his best friend mutilated, incinerated, dead. "Don't come any closer. Go and search around the IED site!"

Out of the settling dust a figure appeared before Captain Tracy, wearing what looked like a flight suit. *A pilot?* he wondered. *Am I dead? Is this where Marine infantry officers go when they die? The Marine Air Wing?* Then, from behind the figure, the muzzle of a 120mm main gun emerged, then the hull of an Abrams tank came into view.

"Sir," the figure before him announced. "It's Tiger zero-two. You told us to race immediately to an explosion. You did that for us. Now we're here for you." The figure was the tank commander of Tiger 02, the call sign for the Abrams. He, like other tankers, wore a suit similar to those that pilots wear.

"Stand by, Tiger zero-two," Tracy said. He turned to see the wreckage of the Humvee. He took a deep breath and lunged toward the third vehicle in the convoy. "Call in an urgent medevac!" he roared. "We've got a mass casualty situation!" He sprinted toward the wreckage, arriving just as Anes discovered the remains of Brown. And as Anes suspected, the blast had killed him instantly.

"Gonzo!" Burke yelled when he found Gonzalez. The explosion had killed him instantly and hurled his body hundreds of feet from the Humvee. Doc Tryon Lippincott, a corpsman with the patrol, dove into saving Wilson.

"Scholl!" Steuter yelled. "SCHOLL!" Anes raced to Steuter's side to help him find Scholl. "Look!" Steuter said. "He's right there." Anes and Steuter sprinted up to a car about a hundred feet from the site of the explosion. The blast had thrown Scholl out of the turret and through the parked car's windshield.

"Mike!" Anes yelled at his close friend. Steuter ripped the door off the car and crawled inside. Scholl gasped for air. Blood streamed down his arms and legs. Steuter and Anes pulled him onto the street.

"We got a Dustoff inbound!" one of the Marines yelled from the third vic in the convoy. Lippincott cut Gunny Wilson free just as Anes lifted Scholl onto Steuter's back. With his friend on his back, he sprinted toward the burning remains of the Humvee.

"You're gonna be okay!" Anes yelled to Scholl. "Your daughter! You're gonna be with your daughter!" The new father continued to gasp for air.

"What LZ is that bird inbound to?" Tracy asked the Marine who had called in the medevac. "I hope not the soccer field! We don't have time to get there!"

"No, sir! Up the road there, there's a clearing, it's about a quarter mile away. I passed the grid."

How we going to get the injured up there? Tracy wondered, then looked over to Tiger 02. "Tiger zero-two!" Tracy yelled, running up to the tank. "We're gonna get the wounded onto the hull and you guys are gonna go as fast as you can up to the top of that hill, where a Dustoff will meet you." The tanker looked at Tracy.

"Okay, sir!"

"Mike, you're gonna live, man!" Anes repeated. "You're gonna live and see Addison!" *This can't be happening,* Anes thought. *He can't die before meeting his daughter!* "Hang on! Hang on, Mike!" *He's only twenty-one, man. This isn't fair. He has to live! This can't be happening!*

Tracy sprinted over to the IED site and helped Lippincott with Wilson. "Let's get him over to the tank!" Tracy surveyed the scene again. "Are there any other survivors?" Only Scholl and Wilson lived.

"Ugh!" Steuter laid Scholl onto the tank hull next to Wilson. Lippincott, on the tank tending to Marcus, immediately started CPR on Scholl. Tracy laid down between the two injured to keep them secure as the Abrams raced to the LZ.

"Go like hell!"

Tiger 02 tore up the hillside as the Dustoff medevac bird flared hard to land in the small field. The tank stopped just a few feet from the Hawk's spinning rotors. Wilson had gone into shock. Scholl stopped breathing. The flight crew secured Wilson first. Tracy carried Scholl to the side of the helicopter. The medics inspected him.

"We can't take him," one said to Tracy. "He's dead."

"He's not dead!" Tracy screamed. "You're taking him, and you're saving him!" The crew secured Mike and continued CPR on him. The captain and Doc Lippincott backed away from rotor wash as the Hawk's engines spun into a scream and the rotors bit into the air.

The Dustoff lifted off the ground and carved an arc to the south. Medics continued CPR on Scholl through the entire flight, then rushed him to waiting surgeons at Al Asad. They fought for him as he struggled to survive. Despite his strength and despite the heroic attempts to save him—by Anes, Steuter, Lippincott, Tracy, Tiger 02, the Dustoff medics, and then the surgeons at Al Asad—Mike Scholl, age twenty-one, died on the operating table. A father to a daughter he'd never meet.

19

RIVER CITY

As surgeons at Al Asad toiled to save Gunny Wilson's life and keep his leg attached, the Marines of the patrol spent the remainder of the day quietly searching for and collecting body parts of their lost friends. The putrid stench of burnt human tissue hung in the air. The fumes stung their noses and bit into their throats. Each breath brought the taste of death. They coughed and wheezed. They searched the IED crater and the roads, buildings, and palm trees surrounding it. They collected chunks of legs, slivers of arms, a foot inside a boot. They found shreds of clothing and gear, some veneered with fire-scorched blood. They placed what they collected in body bags for later DNA identification analysis.

The low sun of late afternoon beamed through a mantle of dense haze. The sky cast a hue of muted yellow onto the Marines, the site of the explosion, and the surrounding buildings, streets, and landscape. The air felt dense. The region remained oddly quiet. No explosions of mortars boomed, no shots of AK-47 fire burst, no IEDs erupted. *I just wish they'd shoot at us so we wouldn't have to keep doing this,* Mario Anes thought. *Why is it so still? So quiet?* Anes thought of Burke, of how he had pushed him away from witnessing Tim Brown, his best friend, just after the explosion. "I'm sorry, man," he said to Burke. "I'm so sorry I kept you from seeing him."

"No, you did the right thing," Burke said. "I appreciate it. Really, I do. It was the right thing to do."

"No," Anes said. "It was wrong. I denied you your last chance to see him. I'm going to regret this for the rest of my life." Anes caught himself. *Stay focused on the job at hand. Keep the apologies for later.*

The patrol returned to the Echo FOB later that night. "Scholl didn't make it," Captain Tracy told them. "We tried."

As soon as 2/3's headquarters learned of the passing of Gonzo, Brown, and then Scholl, it issued a "River City" mandate, prohibiting members of the battalion from any communication, of any type and about any topic, with family and friends. Intended to keep news of the deaths of service members strictly private until families were notified, the void of communication resonated powerfully with friends and family of those deployed—and those in the battalion burning with curiosity of who had died. Back home, when an expected email or phone call didn't arrive, the worry began, grew, and then spread throughout communities of friends and family members of the battalion. In the Triad, 2/3's members knew of the tension and anxiety the communications blackout caused. Each wanted to secretly reach out with an "I'm okay" message. None did, however, always putting the interests of the families of the fallen before their own.

The Echo Marines pondered more than they spoke that night. *No amount of training can prepare you for this,* Mario Anes thought. He dwelled on Scholl, his wife, his daughter he never met. He felt guilt. *I'm a single guy, Mike's age, and he's married and has a daughter. Why him and why not me?* Keeping Burke from seeing his best friend, "Brickhead," also continued to torment him. *I should have allowed him a chance to see him one last time*. Anes and others thought of the horrible moment when the casualty notification teams would be arriving at doorsteps. They thought of the phone calls that would then go out to other family members and to friends. Dennis Gilbert and others of the stay-behind element kept very busy. Very terribly busy.

BACK HOME, CASUALTY Assistant Call Officers, or CACOs, knocked on doors, as they had too many times already for the battalion. Family members passed out in grief. Friends and extended family did what they could to console those closest to fallen Marines, but nothing helped.

Meanwhile, the Marines of Echo, Fox, Golf, and Whiskey prepared for another day.

And AQI fighters seized upon the tragedy, a victory for them, by stepping up their information operations in the area, releasing a shaky video of the detonation that included a clip of Gonzo's ID card that they found in the aftermath, blown hundreds of feet away. They also pressed onward with violent acts, focusing increasingly on Haqlaniyah and Barwana.

"The IED that killed Gonzalez, Brown, and Scholl was one of the biggest set off in this area," Captain Tracy said in the Echo COC after a brief from a Marine explosive ordnance disposal team, members of which had inspected the crater in the wake of the tragedy. "EOD estimates that the IED was composed of roughly six large propane tanks filled with high explosive—six!"

"There's no way they could have put that in there recently," James Steuter said. "They would have needed days to get that much in there."

"Right," Tracy responded. "EOD said that it could have been emplaced over a year ago, with trigger wire attached quickly just in the last few days, which they ran underwater to the Barwana side of the river." Tracy wondered to himself if that was a

Hail Mary of sorts, a lucky shot with a weapon that they'd been waiting to use in a last-ditch push.

Despite the many casualties AQI had inflicted in Haditha to that point—seven Echo Marines and one 1/8 scout sniper killed, and dozens wounded—the nonstop pressure the Marines and attached IP and Iraqi Army units had applied had to be exacting lasting effects on AQI. *Had to be*. He kept those thoughts to himself, however. Victory might be a distant, wan glimmer—might be—but success certainly wasn't yet near at hand.

The company commander decided that he, his Marines, and the IP and the Iraqi Army members attached to the Marines would step up patrols and operations. They would take no rests, despite the catastrophic losses. Every one of Tracy's Marines and officers felt bolstered by the decision. The losses didn't hack at their resolve but strengthened their outlook on winning, on effecting lasting change in memory of the fallen.

20

DYNAMIC AO

SHORTLY AFTER THEIR MOVE TO BAGHDADI AT THE BEGINNING of 2/3's deployment, Whiskey Company saw a dramatic improvement in the security situation in their area. As the Marines conducted operations in the town, they also increasingly pushed patrols farther north, into the Albu Hyatt region, which included the oil-pumping facility called K3. By early November, the battalion sought to move Whiskey from Baghdadi to Albu Hyatt, because intelligence showed a higher use of the area by AQI to support its activities in Haditha, Haqlaniyah, and Barwana.

Tasked with finding the most suitable building for an FOB in the small village from a list drafted by Lieutenant Colonel Donnellan and the battalion's intelligence officer, Captain Paul Bischoff, First Lieutenant Patrick Kinser made a number of forays into a small village. Although he found what he believed to be an ideal location—an abandoned school atop a hill—he needed to pick one from the list given to him. Only one of those locations would work: a local man's house that overlooked the Euphrates. Whereas it was large for a family, the home would prove tiny for a company of Marines. It was also situated mostly in a depression.

But Kinser had no choice. The lieutenant approached the man and explained that he needed to rent the home for six months. The man vehemently objected. Then Kinser produced $40,000 in US cash. The man moved out the next day, and Kinser and Whiskey Marines under his command immediately began reinforcing their new home with sandbags and Hesco barriers—and AQI immediately began attacking.

Day and night, mortars rained onto the new combat outpost (COP). By mid-November the last of Whiskey had departed Baghdadi (replaced by Delta Company of the 3rd Assault Amphibian Battalion), and the company's operations in and around Albu Hyatt were conducted at a blistering pace.

Even though the location of their combat outpost wasn't ideal, Whiskey's move to Albu Hyatt came at the perfect time. As the operational tempo within the core of the Triad, notably in Haditha, kept pressure on AQI, the enemy used Albu Hyatt as a region to dwell, plan, hide, and create IEDs. On patrol after patrol, Whiskey Marines discovered hidden caches of weapons, IED components, and propaganda materials throughout the village and the outlying desert. Squeezed by Echo Company in Haditha, and increasingly pressed by Whiskey, AQI stepped up ground attacks between Albu Hyatt and Haqlaniyah, Golf Company's territory.

Attacks on the FOB in the "Haq," as Golf Company Marines called the town, came at a feverish rate in mid-November. Their FOB was located in a "rats' nest," as Captain Perry Waters, the CO of Golf, described it. AQI attacked and attacked the location with mortars, RPGs, sniper fire, and machine gun ambushes. Sometimes firefights just outside the FOB lasted for four or five hours—Haq was so dense, with so many buildings and structures, AQI had even more tactical options than it did in Haditha. Some firefights began when insurgents attacked the Marines inside the wire of the FOB, and then escalated when they passed into the city, where the Marines were ambushed further. Although the losses mounted for Golf, notably at the beginning of the deployment, with the death of PFC Riviere, and scores were injured in the ensuing months, AQI inflicted its greatest strike just over a week after Echo lost Scholl, Gonzo, and Brown.

On November 22, a mounted patrol consisting of four vehicles passed outside the wire surrounding the Golf FOB. The patrol headed north and entered the Haqlaniyah side of the Bonnie-D neighborhood. By this point, members of the patrol were acclimatized to the frequency and intensity of ambushes in the area, and they also knew of the dangers to the local inhabitants.

CRACK!—CRACK!—CRACK! Shots rang out from at least two positions just as the convoy entered Bonnie-D. But none of the shots hit near the convoy. The patrol leader ordered the vics to head south, where they could dismount and possibly flank the attackers, whereas if they had pressed ahead going north, crossfire might have hit the numerous locals in the area.

As they drove south, an AQI operative hiding in a house two hundred meters to the northwest readied a command wire and a battery. With a slim view of the convoy through the walls and homes before him, he completed the triggering circuit just as the third vehicle—a Humvee—passed over an IED consisting of 150 pounds of explosives.

The blast killed all three Golf Company Marines in the vehicle: twenty-year-old Lance Corporal James Davenport, nineteen-year-old Private Heath Warner, and Lance Corporal Joshua Alonzo, who had just turned twenty-one years old less than three weeks earlier.

ANOTHER RIVER CITY call went out. More CACO visits ensued. Lieutenant Colonel Donnellan, Sergeant Major Wilkinson, and Captain Perry made more phone calls and wrote more emails of condolences. Captain Tracy pondered both Bonnie-D IED strikes. *Were there more massive IEDs hidden? How long had the IED that killed Alonzo, Warner, and Davenport been buried? When would the next one erupt? Was this a second Hail Mary strike—the second and last one? Was this a sign of desperation, or was AQI actually gaining the upper hand in the fight?* The phantom enemy proved ever more elusive—so much so that its status proved impossible to gauge. *Were they ready to collapse, or on the cusp of tripling or quadrupling their efforts?*

The population remained cowed, oppressed and intimidated by AQI. They feared embracing the Americans, despite the Marines' overtures of friendship and opportunity. Images of naked, bludgeoned, and decapitated bodies hanging from street lights and heads of family, friends, and neighbors planted on stakes at major intersections were burned into their memories. The Americans promised a brighter future, and they proved their resolve with the blood of their own ranks, but the leaden, dark mantle of fear hung low over the Triad.

The IED attacks in Bonnie-D didn't just kill and maim Americans; they reinforced a message to the locals: Side with us, or face death. *If we can do this to them, think of what we can do to you.*

AQI AGAIN INFLICTED death on the battalion three days after the November 22 Bonnie-D IED strike that killed Alonzo, Davenport, and Warner. Ballistic glass protected guard posts at the FOBs in Haditha, Barwana, and Haqlaniyah, allowing Marines standing guard a safe, unobstructed view. But RCT-7 had yet to deliver the protective shield to the new FOB at Albu Hyatt.

CRACK! A single gunshot split the quiet of Albu Hyatt on the night of November 25. Thud!

Kinser bolted up to the roof of the compound and found twenty-year-old Lance Corporal Jeromy West laid out flat. Kinser began CPR, but the AQI sniper had shot him in the head.

A Navy Corpsman attached to Whiskey Company pronounced West dead.

DESPITE THE LOSSES AQI had inflicted on the battalion, Lieutenant Colonel Donnellan and Major Trane McCloud saw not only progress but also a solid path to victory—if only they could proceed with their three Bs plan. They just needed buy-in from RCT-7.

But Colonel Crowe rebuffed the idea of a complete berm around the Triad. He wanted to conserve assets and only berm those "essential areas" of the Triad. While the commander decried the situation on the ground in 2/3's AO, Donnellan and his staff tried to convince the RCT to support the much larger berm plan. With the RCT Operations Officer unconvinced that the expanded berm would be worth the additional time and assets, Donnellan's only option was to try to convince the commander directly. They decided to brief Crowe on the plan in person. Donnellan and McCloud arranged to fly to Al Asad to meet with Colonel Crowe and his staff on the third of December.

21

★

TO THE BREAKING POINT

On the morning of December 3, 2006, Lieutenant Colonel Jim Donnellan, Major Trane McCloud, intelligence specialist Corporal Joshua Sticklen, and thirteen other passengers walked up the loading ramp of a CH-46E Sea Knight "Phrog" helicopter at the landing zone atop the Haditha Dam. With all secured on the aircraft's bench seats, the pilot on the controls of the aircraft, call sign "Sexton 32," lifted the Phrog into the sky and then nosed it into forward flight. WHIRRRR! A high-pitched howl screeched from one of the turboshaft engines just as the helicopter crossed over the northern wall of the dam. The engine had ingested a small chunk of concrete, which lodged in one of its compressor vanes. The engine shut down. Pilots and crew (and passengers) know the twin-engine, tandem rotor CH-46 to be an underpowered helicopter—underpowered with *both* engines running. Sexton 32 now had just one.

The Phrog careened nose-first toward the north wall of the dam. With just a second to spare, the pilot activated the working engine's emergency throttle, allowing more fuel to dump into its guts and blast additional power to the rotors. He pitched the nose of the aircraft toward the sky just before it collided with the wall. With the forward half of the Phrog clear, the pilot wrestled the controls to raise the tail end of the helicopter over the wall. *WHUMP!* The rear landing gear slammed into the crown of the dam. Sexton 32 careened nose-first toward the water, fifty feet below.

The pilot leveled the Phrog's attitude just before impact. SMACK! Water exploded outward from the helicopter as it hit the surface of Lake Qadisiyah. "Egress! Egress! Egress!" one of the crew chiefs roared, fearing the collective weight of all the passengers would be too much for one engine to handle. The pilot fought to keep the helicopter level—if it rocked too far to one side, water would pour through a gun door and the aircraft would disappear below the surface in seconds, drowning all. All passengers unbuckled their seat belts and stood, ready to leap as the pilot began "water taxiing" the helicopter, operating it as a de facto hovercraft, an emergency procedure.

"JUMP!" the crew chief yelled. "JUMP INTO THE WATER!"

Donnellan ditched his flak jacket and gear rack. He looked up to see Trane McCloud standing directly opposite him. With his helmet still donned and clutching his service rifle, Donnellan dove into Lake Qadisiyah. He lunged for the concrete shore as his muscles seized in the icy December water. Gasping, he threw his rifle to the side—but it caught on his holstered sidearm. Others who had reached safety dropped all their gear and raced back into the lake to help those swimming ashore. Donnellan spun around to check on McCloud. The operations officer had made it out of the helicopter. Donnellan closed on the shore. *Fifty feet. Forty feet.* The frigid water sapped his energy with each lunge. His heart pounded. He gasped for air.

A few seconds later Donnellan looked back again to check on McCloud. The operations officer had vanished. Donnellan shot glances to the left, then to the right. *Nothing.* He pressed onward, then crawled onto the angled concrete. The battalion commander and others searched feverishly for McCloud and the three others who hadn't reached safety: Corporal Joshua Sticklen, Army Specialist Dustin Adkins of the 5th Special Forces Group, and Air Force Captain Kermit Evans of the 27th Civil Engineer Squadron. The four never emerged. All had drowned in the cold water, pulled into the depths by the weight of their gear.

Another River City call flashed through the Triad. All in the battalion wondered who had died—and how. Details soon emerged, spread first by those who witnessed the events at the dam, and then by secondary and tertiary sources. These details included the fact that the battalion's operations officer, one of the unit's key staff members, had perished. "That wasn't supposed to happen, man," said a junior Marine. "Officers aren't supposed to die, especially officers that high up in the battalion." Families and friends of the fallen learned the fates of those lost within hours.

"My wife told me that she had written me off, that she never expected me to return," said a junior officer in the battalion. "She grieved for all those lost, officers and enlisted, equally. But she was under the mindset, right or wrong, that when officers die, then the situation is beyond bad. McCloud dying knocked the wind out of her," he said. "It showed that anybody could die in the AO. The enemy and fate were indiscriminate."

A FEW HOURS after the CH-46 plunged over the edge of the Haditha Dam into Lake Qadisiyah, a group of Iraqi children rushed out of class at a small school just north of Haditha. Their school day over, they headed home along a meandering dirt road occasionally used by Marines, Iraqi Police, and Iraqi Army units.

CLICK.

One of the students had stepped on a patch of dirt covering a pressure plate. BOOM! The explosion slashed the group of children with searing hot shrapnel. The blast tore off arms and legs, shattered bones, ripped eyes, and crushed skulls.

Second Lieutenant Ben Early heard the blast from a vehicle control point a couple miles to the south of the carnage. He and others stared silently to the north for a moment. They waited for the radio to erupt in a torrent of requests for reinforcements and medevacs. Silence. Then, within twenty minutes, locals began to arrive with the children, pleading for help from the Marines. Although the people feared AQI, they knew that AQI had caused the massacre and at that point didn't care about the terrorists' threats of decapitation and dismemberment and death—they just wanted to save their children.

A father, crying, pleaded with the Marines to save his young daughter. Her legs torn off, she barely breathed. Then another father, holding his son's limp body, approached. Within minutes, ten local vehicles had converged at the small outpost.

"There's no time for a Dustoff," Early said, helping a corpsman tend to the children's wounds. The lieutenant radioed a Marine Corps UH-1N "Huey" gunship that had been patrolling the area with a Marine AH-1W SuperCobra gunship. The Huey, while fitted for a ground attack mission, could nevertheless carry passengers. "Young children!" Early yelled. The Huey touched down and the Marines loaded as many injured children as the aircraft could hold. The helicopter lifted off and sped toward Al Asad.

Some children died en route. Surgeons could save only a handful. The scene at the checkpoint ranked as the most gruesome, horrific, and nightmarish any of the Marines and corpsmen had ever witnessed. Echo Marines Max Draper, Mike Dowling, and others, covered in the children's blood from trying to help save them, now tried to console the fathers of the lost children.

IN HADITHA, A young girl riding a bicycle approached a squad of Echo Marines. They noticed her Mickey Mouse backpack. They smiled at her and she laughed as she pedaled past them.

BOOM! The backpack had been filled with hand grenades daisy-chained together to form an IED. She hadn't understood her instructions to press a button when she got close to the Americans, so the AQI operative triggered the bomb remotely. Unscathed by the blast, the Marines lunged toward the bicycle, hoping to help the little girl. The blast had ripped her body to shreds, however, killing her instantly.

Captain Tracy pondered how the situation could get any worse. Although the IED that had killed the children near the northern checkpoint may have been intended for a Marine Convoy, the terrorists had nevertheless set it near a school, without regard to the safety of children. *Children.*

And in Haditha, AQI were now using children as remote-controlled suicide bombers.

"SIR," ECHO COMPANY Marine Sergeant Eric Ciotola said over the radio to Matt Tracy later that day. "There's a man here with information about the IED that killed all those kids."

"And," Tracy responded.

"He has the name of the guy who put in the bomb. And he showed me where he lives on a map."

"Who brought him in?" Tracy asked. "Did the Iraqi Army question him?"

"No, sir," Ciotola responded. "He just came in on his own. In broad daylight." Ciotola paused. "He's the father of one of the children that the blast killed. He said he's sick of all of this. He's thanking all of us for trying to save his daughter. Everyone in his small village is sick of all of this killing. They can't take it anymore, killing all those children put them over the edge. They're not afraid of Al Qaeda anymore. They want to help us—without us asking them to help us."

Born in unspeakable tragedy, the "Haditha Awakening" had begun.

22

═ ★ ═

SHIFTING WINDS OF
PERSEVERANCE AND STRENGTH

THE BATTALION'S LOSSES WEIGHED MORE HEAVILY ON JIM DON-
nellan than he'd ever reveal. After the helicopter accident at
the dam, the number of 2/3's fallen stood at seventeen, including Trane McCloud, with whom the battalion commander had
worked so hard to craft a path toward victory. The two had also
forged a close friendship. From a personal perspective, he felt
intensely for the families, friends, and fellow Marines of those
of the battalion killed and injured. From a professional standpoint, he knew how crippling losses due to death and wounds
could prove to a military campaign. *Could.* More importantly,
he understood how perseverance and strength—at all levels,
from senior battalion command to the fire team—could well
overcome these losses.

Donnellan and Sergeant Major Wilkinson not only recognized this and constantly encouraged this throughout the battalion, they continued to demonstrate it. And in early December,
this perseverance and strength, which had been a foundation

for all those in the Triad fight, yielded much more than a glimmer of the hope Captain Tracy had envisioned just weeks prior.

"Synergy!" Captain Matt Tracy said to Captain Billy Parker in early December. "Synergy!" Tracy visited Parker in the CMOC, or Civil-Military Operations Center, located adjacent to the Echo FOB in Haditha. Almost overnight, enemy attacks had fallen off a cliff and discoveries of weapons and IED caches greatly increased in the Triad. Some of the finds stupefied members of the battalion.

In Haditha, the Whiskey Company platoon attached to Echo discovered a hide containing RPG launchers, cell phones, artillery shells, two-way radios, cameras, AK-47s, machine guns, submachine guns, shotguns, pistols, thousands of rounds of ammunition—even two swords.

In Haqlaniyah, Golf Company unearthed a cache containing dynamite, detonation cord, "Bangalore Torpedoes" (cylindrical charges used for clearing obstacles but used by AQI for making IEDs), hundreds of mortar and artillery rounds, thousands of rounds of AK-47 ammunition, dozens of AK-47s and machine guns, and dozens of IED batteries and other IED implements.

In another raid, Golf Company found dozens of AK-47s, explosives, video cameras for recording IED strikes, nine fake Iraqi passports, binoculars, pistols, and spools of copper wire for IED triggers. Echo Company, searching the desert area west of Haditha, discovered a football-field-sized area containing multiple caches and a large room located thirty feet underground containing tons of explosives, mortar rounds, artillery rounds, AK-47s, machine guns, ammunition, suicide vests, RPG launchers, RPG rounds, and various materials to craft IED initiators.

The Marines, IP, and Iraqi Army didn't just find weapons and materials, they also arrested dozens of Al Qaeda and suspected AQI enablers. In Barwana, Marine scout snipers found and killed Bilal Maiz, the AQI shooter who killed Fox Company's Edwardo Lopez.

Working with the IP—throughout the AO—yielded reams of actionable intelligence. Each successful raid then paid yet more dividends. Daily acts by the Americans, like those of Early and his Marines after the IED attack on the children, won the trust of the people of the region. The population, sick of the violence, terror, and fear wrought by Al Qaeda, began coming forth with information about the group on their own. The number of these "walk-ins" skyrocketed in the first weeks of December.

Billy Parker, working closely with Matt Tracy, the Marines of Echo Company, and the IP and Iraqi Army in Haditha, laid the groundwork for a renewed government, municipal services, and businesses. "Don't eat at the chow hall!" Captain Tracy repeatedly ordered. "Buy food from local businesses! Anything you need, buy it locally!" Stores opened, locals began crowding streets, municipal services began functioning again, and schools reopened. Captain Tracy and Echo Marines conducted regular "operations" to buy plumbing supplies, hardware, food, even basic electronics.

At the battalion's very darkest moment, with so many killed and wounded—so many lives changed forever—the collective toil of the members of 2/3 was showing results. They had done it all, from working with IP to kicking in doors and handing out candy dressed in costumes, and now they saw the first signs of success.

But was it just a lull? "We're gonna double our efforts," Captain Tracy instructed his Marines. "This is just the beginning."

Even Colonel Crowe, seemingly bent on relieving Captain Tracy, recognized the change. He approved the plan Trane McCloud and Jim Donnellan had developed—and provided support for it in the form of heavy equipment and more BATS sets. Berming operations began throughout the core of the Triad. The Marines reinforced entry control points and vehicle control points. Working with Billy Parker and the CMOC, the Marines issued ID cards and driver licenses. Commerce returned. People congregated. Children played soccer in the streets. The Triad seemed to be turning a corner.

But had the Marines and their Iraqi partners defeated AQI? An army of phantoms, Al Qaeda had proved to be an enemy simultaneously everywhere and nowhere. On the attack, operatives came at the Marines everywhere, but during counterattacks, they disappeared. Nowhere to be found. And then they'd strike again.

"SIR," LIEUTENANT KINSER said to the visiting lieutenant colonel at the Whiskey FOB in Albu Hyatt. "You'd better put your ballistic goggles on, sir, and then come inside." The lieutenant colonel had been surveying Marine Corps operations in Al Anbar Province to compile a status report for a higher command.

The officer barked back, reminding Kinser that lieutenants don't tell lieutenant colonels what to do.

"Sir, while it doesn't happen every time a convoy comes inside the wire, it is a cue for the enemy to attack," Kinser responded. "They know that once everyone dismounts, it's a big target for mortars. I'm just telling you for your own safety."

BOOM! Just after Kinser explained the danger, an 82mm mortar sailed inside the wire, exploding just twenty feet from the group of them.

Blood poured from the lieutenant colonel's left eye and left leg.

BOOM! A second mortar exploded. BOOM! Then a third. The group sprinted inside the FOB. The lieutenant colonel went into shock. BOOM! BOOM! Two more mortars struck, slamming into the visiting convoy's Humvees. An urgent Dust-off request went out. Minutes later, Kinser and other Whiskey Marines carried the lieutenant colonel to the LZ outside the FOB's entrance.

Although enemy activity had slowed dramatically in the core of the Triad, AQI continued its reign of terror in the Albu Hyatt region. In Haditha, Haqlaniyah, and Barwana, the fight was for the allegiance of the people; in Albu Hyatt, Al Qaeda simply wanted the Marines out so that operatives could use the area as a staging ground for their operations in the heart of the Triad. AQI attacked primarily with mortars and IEDs, notably IEDs set on MSR Bronze, which connected Albu Hyatt with the core of the Triad to the north, and with Baghdadi and Al Asad to the south.

The battalion sent a large, nine-vehicle convoy to Albu Hyatt the following day to recover the Humvees damaged in the mortar attack and to resupply the Golf Company FOB. BOOM! An IED hit the sixth vehicle, a seven-ton, causing no damage. A few miles closer to Albu Hyatt, however, another IED struck the lead vehicle, also a seven-ton, destroying it and injuring a number of Marines, one of whom required an urgent Dustoff medevac. The convoy towed back to the dam not only the two Humvees damaged in the mortar attack but also the destroyed seven-ton.

As the berms went up around Haditha, Haqlaniyah, and Barwana, and as the population awakened to orient themselves to building a resurgent government and economy, AQI had clearly focused on Whiskey and the Albu Hyatt region. Just days after the IED hit the nine-vehicle convoy twice, the terrorist group lashed out again.

Driving a Humvee toward Haqlaniyah along MSR Bronze, Lance Corporal Matthew Clark didn't see the expertly laid command wire. AQI had begun using a new means to hide IEDs: it put them in paved roads using gasoline. The process began with someone inconspicuously marking a location with a rock or a stick. Then a second person would drive to that location with a specially modified car that had an access port in the floor. They'd open the access port and pour gasoline on the marked location and a narrow pathway leading to the side of the road. Later, after the gasoline had softened the asphalt, AQI operatives would dig out the asphalt, plant an IED, and then lay command wire under the strip leading to the IED's location. They'd repack the surface with the removed blacktop, extend the command wire a couple hundred meters to a hide site, and then wait.

Clark's Humvee, which carried him and two other Whiskey Marines, was completely destroyed in the explosion. He died on scene. An urgent Dustoff spun up and saved the other two, who suffered multiple fractured bones and penetration wounds.

23

★

CHRISTMAS

"GOT 'EM!" FIRST LIEUTENANT JAMES "JJ" KONSTANT SAID, EYE-ing five men emplacing an IED on MSR Bronze. It was Christmas Eve. He viewed the men from twenty thousand feet above, courtesy of a Marine Corps F/A-18D Hornet of Marine All-Weather Fighter Attack Squadron 242 (VMFA [AW]-242), the "Bats." Based at Al Asad, the Hornet, one of two in formation supporting Konstant and Whiskey Company that night, used its targeting pod to capture the imagery. The pod, controlled from the cockpit by a WSO (pronounced "wizz-oh"), or weap-ons systems officer, imaged the men using its thermal infrared scanner, a sensor that responds to energy given off as heat. The WSO, in the rear seat of the cockpit, then downlinked the feed to Konstant, who watched the black-and-white imagery on a computer screen in the COC of Whiskey's FOB in Albu Hyatt. Konstant watched the video and communicated with the WSO courtesy of a "ROVER," a Remotely Operated Video Enhanced Receiver. The system allowed Konstant to see, in near real time, what the pod imaged and to speak with the WSO.

In addition to targeting pods, the two Hornets carried laser-guided bombs, explosive-tipped rockets, and 20mm high-explosive rounds for their high-speed multibarrel rotary M61 Vulcan cannons. With hostile intent positively identified, Konstant requested permission from 2/3's air officer for the Hornets to engage the AQI operatives with bombs and strafing runs. In order for the battalion to employ aviation attack assets, however, RCT-7 needed to approve the strike.

Minutes passed.

The AQI members continued to emplace the IED. The Hornets orbited above, scanning. Konstant stared at the computer screen. "Come on," he said. Lieutenant Patrick Kinser stood behind him, his eyes also glued on the enemy at work. "Come on," JJ repeated. "Approve the strike."

"Christmas Eve," Kinser said to Konstant.

"I know," Konstant said. "If they don't approve the strike, then we have to send out a patrol to get these guys—"

"—Christmas Eve," Kinser repeated. With the IED placed in the road and trigger wire attached, the AQI operatives tossed the first concealing shovel loads of dirt onto it. Despite the myriad "eyes" looking for AQI activity, from unmanned aircraft to targeting pods, patrols, and scout sniper teams, the Marines simply lacked the observational coverage to keep an eye on all the nooks in their large AO. Konstant, who had survived a massive IED strike just weeks earlier, knew that a patrol sent to interdict the IED being placed could hit another that AQI had set earlier.

"The last thing we want," Konstant said, "is for a casualty notification team to come Christmas morning." He paused. "Come on, approve the strike."

Konstant and Kinser continued to stare at the thermal images of the men finishing the placement of the IED. The Hornets continued to circle twenty thousand feet above. They'd need to soon "break station" to fly to a Marine Corps KC-130J Super Hercules for in-flight refueling. "Where's that approval . . . "

RCT-7 denied the request.

The Hornets shot away for fuel as Konstant and Kinser launched a three-vehicle quick reaction force. The AQI operatives patted the last of the asphalt atop the massive IED they had just buried.

The explosion came minutes later. Approaching MSR Bronze from a side road, the lead Humvee of the QRF hit a pressure-plate IED that had been buried earlier. Captain Capuzzi, who had been on another patrol bringing hot food to Marines manning entry control points and vehicle control points, heard the blast. So did all those at the Albu Hyatt FOB, including Konstant and Kinser. The two lieutenants feared the worst.

"Lead vic hit a pressure-plate IED," one of the Marines of the QRF transmitted.

Kinser and Konstant put in an urgent Dustoff request. The Army aviators and medics, as they had so many times before, sprinted to one of their Hawks at Al Asad. Once off the ground, they raced through the desert air to save lives and limbs. The blast severely injured the vehicle commander and the gunner. By the time the Dustoff landed, the driver, twenty-one-year-old Lance Corporal Stephen Morris, had died.

"PROFANE FIVE-FOUR AND five-five checking in," the voice announced over the ROVER system in Whiskey's COC. It was Christmas night. The transmission announced that a "section" (two aircraft) of Hornets, call signs Profane 54 and Profane 55, had arrived to support Whiskey's efforts. The Bats used "Profane" as their call sign throughout their August 2006 to February 2007 deployment to Al Asad.

"Roger," Konstant responded. The death of Stephen Morris weighed heavily on the lieutenant's mind that night. "Got you, Profane."

After the initial check-in, the Hornet section passed Konstant basic information about their flight. "We're Angels two-zero," the WSO of Profane 54 announced, indicating that they flew at an altitude of twenty thousand feet above sea level. He then radioed their location and listed the munitions they carried: Between the two aircraft, they flew with four GBU-12 500-pound laser-guided bombs and four GBU-38 500-pound JDAM (Joint Defense Attack Munition) GPS-guided bombs. They also carried a total of ten 5-inch-diameter "Zuni" rockets with high-explosive warheads in wing-mounted pods. Each Hornet also carried the standard load of 500 rounds of "20 mike-mike HEI," or 20mm high-explosive incendiary rounds. HEI rounds explode on impact and spray shrapnel in all directions, with a kill radius similar to that of a hand grenade—but fired at a rate of approximately 100 per second.

Then the WSO of Profane gave Konstant one of the most important pieces of information to those on the ground supported by aviation assets: time "on station," meaning how long the Hornets could loiter above them. "Zero plus three-zero on station," meaning thirty minutes. The WSO followed that with "We have our flying gas station not too far away, though, so we can hang out all night for you guys. We just need to make gas runs every thirty mikes."

The aviators, crew, and maintainers of the Bats, a storied Marine Corps squadron, had all learned the news of Stephen Morris. Just as it weighed heavily on Konstant—and others of Whiskey and the battalion at large—members of the squadron pledged to do whatever it took to continue to support the ground fight Whiskey waged.

"Controlling air," the colloquialism for ground personnel guiding aviation assets to perform specific acts, from using their sensors to scan an area to releasing ordnance, ranks as one of the most difficult and critical roles in the world of modern warfare. The role traditionally called "FACs," or forward air controllers, the Marine Corps tasked exclusively to actual pilots of any type of aircraft. In late 2005, the Marine Corps began training non-pilot officers (all Marine Corps pilots must be commissioned officers) to control air. Called JTACs (pronounced "jay-tacks"), or Joint Terminal Attack Controllers, these personnel supported the workload of forward air controllers. (The Marine Corps continued to use the term *FAC*, although technically all FACs are JTACs. Furthermore, JTAC is a "joint" or interservice term. JTACs of all services train to the same standards.)

JJ Konstant and a number of other lieutenants of 2/3 participated in a JTAC course in Norfolk, Virginia, then conducted a number of "controls" during live fire training at Naval Air Station Fallon, in northern Nevada. Although well versed in "JTAC-ese" from a number of battles in which he participated during 2/3's Afghan deployment, where he worked with others carefully coordinating close air support missions, his training at Norfolk and then at Fallon intimately familiarized him with the myriad factors involved with coordinating aviation assets. After Profane 54 and 55 checked in on station, Konstant directed the jets to begin a sweep of the area, beginning with MSR Bronze.

Marvels of aerospace technology, targeting pods include a visible wavelength "TV" scanner that provides color imagery (at wavelengths visible to the human eye, from violet to red) and thermal infrared. Both the TV and the thermal IR sensors are stabilized for rock-solid imagery, and both can zoom to great degrees, bringing a "super telephoto" view of any area in direct line of sight—and from twenty thousand feet during clear weather, that's any subject not concealed. Targeting pods also include infrared laser "pointers" to "sparkle" a subject on the ground, drawing the attention of any other party, in the air or on the ground able to visualize infrared laser beams, to a feature, target, or location. Pods also include the vital laser designator. The designator emits a powerful beam at a user-specified frequency. With the designator aimed at a target, a laser-guided bomb or missile, with the frequency of the laser beam emitted by the designator programmed into it, flies toward the target using the laser light reflected off of it.

"Right there," Konstant transmitted to Profane 54's WSO over ROVER. "Can you zoom in on that bongo truck?" Working closely with the pilot on the controls of Profane 54, the Hornet's WSO slewed the thermal IR sensor and zoomed it in on a small cargo truck, called a "bongo truck" by the Marines, traveling along MSR Bronze.

"Pretty late for pizza delivery," Kinser remarked. He had just joined Konstant in the Whiskey COC.

"Yeah," Konstant said. The truck slowed and turned onto the road on which the IED had killed Morris less than twenty-four hours earlier. It passed the explosion's crater, continued for another fifty meters, then stopped.

"We got a Scan Eagle coming our way," Kinser said, reading a mIRC message sent from 2/3's air officer. The Scan Eagle, an unmanned aircraft with a wingspan of just over ten feet, had been "pushed" to the area by RCT-7 to keep tabs on Whiskey's activities. Flying much lower than the Hornets, the Scan Eagle also collected real-time visible wavelength and thermal infrared imagery.

"The operator at Al Asad better be prepared to get Crowe's personal 'eye in the sky' out of the way if we need to employ those Hornets," Kinser said.

"Looks like more coming to the pizza party," Konstant said. A sedan and two motorcycles converged on the bongo truck.

"These guys are bold," Kinser said.

"Or desperate," Konstant responded. Within minutes, seven men began digging a large hole in the dirt road. Then they unloaded a large object from the truck.

"Okay, that's P-I-D," Kinser said, a reference to positive identification of hostile intent. "They're digging a hole for an IED and that's the device right there. They just offloaded it from the truck."

"I'm not going to waste any time with this," Konstant said. "These are probably the same guys who put in the IED that went off last night."

"Scan Eagle's on station," Kinser read off the mIRC screen.

"Great," Konstant responded. "Just in time to get in the way of the Hornets attacking these guys."

The unmanned aerial vehicle (UAV) was flying low so its small, low-power sensors could capture usable imagery. To eliminate the chance of a collision, its operators at Al Asad would need to push the aircraft out of the way for the Hornets to descend to use their rockets or guns, a procedure called "deconflicting."

"We're gonna need to engage these guys," Konstant transmitted to Profane 54's WSO.

Suddenly, the men on the ground split into two groups just after the Scan Eagle arrived. Although the distant sounds of the Hornets' engines may have reached the terrorists, spooking them, they were more likely alerted by the distinctive buzzing sound of the gasoline "pusher" engine on the rear of the UAV flying low in the cold, dense, still air of the late December night.

"Okay," Kinser barked at the ROVER screen. "We can't let these guys get away."

The bongo truck sped off, dragging the IED behind it. Seconds later, as the sedan and motorcycles raced away in the opposite direction, the truck slammed to a halt. Three men emerged and tossed the IED back inside the truck, then turned around and returned to the dig site, stopped, and then continued in the direction of the sedan and the two motorcycles.

"Profane five-four," Konstant transmitted, "request that you engage the bongo truck first, which is in trace of the sedan and two motorcycles." Konstant then transmitted a "6-line" brief to Profane 54's WSO. An abbreviated form of a "9-line brief," the 6-line gives an aircraft a set of instructions to conduct an attack on a ground target.

Profane 54 was positioned for an effective drop. The WSO input a laser frequency into the targeting pod's designator and one of the GBU-12 laser-guided bombs. Profane 55 requested the operators of the Scan Eagle to move the UAV to the north of the engagement area, then broke formation with Profane 54. Profane 55 circled around to set up for a rocket and gun run.

"Profane five-four," Konstant transmitted, "you're cleared hot." The cleared hot call gave the okay to the aircraft to engage the target.

"Roger," the WSO of Profane 54 transmitted to Konstant.

Both lieutenants in the Whiskey COC glared at the ROVER screen.

The weapons systems officer placed the laser on the bongo truck, then "led" it slightly by aiming ahead of the moving vehicle. Because of miniscule delays between directional adjustments and the resultant trajectory of a guided bomb of any type, operators of designators needed to adjust their aim for moving targets, gauging where the targets will be at the moment the bomb hits the ground—otherwise, a munition hits where a target *was* a fraction of a second prior to impact. "Thirty seconds," the WSO said. Profane 54 "kicked up" slightly in altitude with the release of the GBU-12.

Kinser and JJ watched the bongo truck jostle along the dirt road.

"Twenty seconds."

The truck slowed, then sped up.

"Ten seconds."

The lieutenants stopped breathing and blinking their eyes and craned their necks closer to the ROVER monitor. The screen "whited out" as the bomb exploded. The WSO zoomed out to give a wider field of view. The plume from the bomb roiled into the night sky from the impact point—about fifty feet behind the bongo truck. But that was close enough. JJ and Kinser watched the vehicle fishtail, then crash to a stop on the side of the dirt road. Four men staggered out and began running as a confused group, searching for cover. It was too late.

"Profane five-five, you're cleared hot," Konstant said after another 6-line brief.

Profane 55 nosed into an attack dive with its crosshairs on the group. Three Zunis blasted from the Hornet's rocket pod, slamming into ground next to the foursome.

"Beautiful," Kinser said, smiling. "Delicious."

As Profane 54 set up for a bomb drop on the sedan and the motorcycles, Profane 55 quickly switched over to the 20mm gun.

"Profane five-five, you're cleared hot for twenty mike-mike," Konstant transmitted.

BRRRR! A half second's worth of 20mm high-explosive rounds blasted downrange as the pilot of the Hornet pulled out of the dive. The high-explosive rounds erupted around the remains of the four Al Qaeda members. The attack shredded them. Konstant then cleared hot Profane 54 for another GBU-12 laser-guided bomb drop.

"Thirty seconds," Profane 54's WSO calmly announced, the crosshairs just ahead of the sedan and two motorcycles.

"Profane five-five," Konstant transmitted, "request you reduce that bongo truck as we believe it to be carrying improvised explosive devices."

"Reduce it to nothing," Kinser said, grinning. Konstant transmitted another 6-line brief followed by another cleared hot call.

"Roger," Profane 55's WSO transmitted.

"Twenty seconds," Profane 54's WSO said, counting down to the second GBU-12 drop. "Ten seconds."

BOOM! The laser-guided bomb hit within twenty meters of all three vehicles. As Profane 55 prepared for a drop of a GBU-38 JDAM on the stationary bongo truck, 54 circled around and nosed into an attack dive, aiming for three AQI members who had survived the bomb strike.

"Cleared hot."

A gun run immediately followed a salvo of Zunis. Glowing AQI body parts littered the ROVER screen.

"Thirty seconds," Profane 55's WSO announced.

A half minute later the JDAM careened into the bongo truck. BOOM! The massive explosion shook the Albu Hyatt FOB.

"That much less explosives they have to use," Kinser said.

The JDAM's blast set off what EOD later estimated to be hundreds of pounds of explosives inside the bongo truck. The

ROVER view of the strike grew wider as Profane 55 linked up with 54 and the two oriented on the "flying gas station." The screen went blank.

Kinser grinned. Konstant sat stone-faced. Colonel Crowe already had his staff opening an investigation into Konstant for the use of the jets without "proper authorization."

A FEW HOURS after the dust settled and twisted metal cooled around the chunks of AQI operatives in the silent desert outside of Albu Hyatt, a van slowly maneuvered through the suburban streets of Lake Jackson, Texas.

A half a world away from the Triad, the van parked in front of the home of Lance Corporal Stephen Morris's parents. The Christmas morning visitors, a casualty notification team, knocked on the front door. . . .

"OKAY, LET'S MOVE," Lieutenant Ben Early said to his squad. Early, dressed as Santa Claus, led a patrol of Echo Marine "elves" outside the wire on Christmas morning. Each carried a large sack slung over his shoulder containing wrapped presents, food, candy, school supplies, clothing, stuffed animals, and medical aids. The elves also carried stacks of leaflets that Captains Tracy and Billy Parker had created and then reproduced on their ditto machine that explained the occasion and further reinforced the intentions of the Americans in the region.

The outpouring of support by the families and friends of Echo in the weeks between Operation Halloween in Haditha and Christmas had been nearly overwhelming. Costumes arrived, gifts arrived, wrapping paper and tape arrived, candy arrived, food arrived—anything and everything those back home felt would be appreciated arrived. Families and friends of the members of the battalion held drives among neighbors, at places of work, at schools, and at churches. Christmas Day patrols throughout the city delivered all of it—over two thousand pounds' worth.

AQI could do nothing. It didn't fire a single shot on Christmas Day in Haditha, or in Barwana. A couple AQI operatives squeezed off a handful of AK-47 rounds in Haqlaniyah at a patrol of Marines and Iraqi Police. The harassment fire, however, barely harassed. The attack didn't cause a scratch of damage. The collective outlook of the people in the area had transitioned from facedown and cowed by AQI to heads up and looking forward to rebuilding lives in a city ravaged by war.

24

★

AT WAR WITH A SPREADSHEET AND A MAP

THE MARINES AND THEIR ATTACHED IP AND IRAQI ARMY patrols continued to identify and detain AQI operatives and find caches of their weapons and supplies throughout the Triad in the days following Christmas. One discovery, by Golf Company in Haqlaniyah, netted hundreds of pounds of explosives, RPG launchers, and AK-47s and dozens of full magazines, rockets, mortars, mines, and piles of propaganda materials.

Every day, more children showed up for school, more shops opened, and more local men volunteered to join the Iraqi Police force. Colonel Farouk continued to work with Captains Billy Parker and Matt Tracy to reach out to local sheiks to win their steadfast allegiance for the nascent government and to help oppose any overtures or initiatives of any kind by Al Qaeda. In short, the confluence of the battalion's efforts—from the three Bs plan, to working with Colonel Farouk and his dedicated IP, consistent patrolling, and, most importantly, having the right attitude in dealing with the local population—had AQI bloodied and seemingly ready to crumble in what was their last strong-hold in Iraq.

Colonel Crowe departed and Matt Tracy remained the company commander, as his Marines continued to win multiple fights in the city of Haditha. Part of a preordained rotation cycle, Regimental Combat Team 2 (RCT-2), led by Colonel H. Stacy Clardy, relieved-in-place RCT-7 in early January 2007. Clardy immediately proved to be an enabler, an operational ally, a "force multiplier" for all components of 2/3. On a number of occasions, Clardy even accompanied Colonel Donnellan and Sergeant Major Wilkinson outside the wire on their Jump CP journeys around the AO.

Despite the dramatic turn of events for the battalion, the Marines knew that the enemy maintained a vicious outlook. Throughout the war, AQI had proved to be dynamic and adaptable. Although Al Qaeda struck only a couple times in the week following Christmas, once with a tossed hand grenade and once with a small IED (both in Haqlaniyah, and neither causing as much as a scratch), intelligence reports showed that it had moved the majority of what remained of its capability to the desert surrounding Albu Hyatt.

Was AQI trying to rest and regroup? Was it waiting for reinforcements from Syria and other countries? None in the battalion, and none in any higher command in Iraq, knew with any certainty. At that point, AQI in senior positions likely didn't even have much of a plan other than to inflict as much damage as possible on their way out as a force in the country. The Marines of the battalion, as they had throughout the deployment, would continue to adapt to Al Qaeda's tactics.

DESPITE BEING A part of the greater Haditha Triad, Whiskey's area of operation differed in many ways from those of the other line companies of the battalion. Whereas dense urban terrain defined much of Haditha, Barwana, and Haqlaniyah, Whiskey's

AO was composed mostly of open desert and small hamlets on the shores of the Euphrates. The intel that drove most of the successful operations in the core of the Triad, notably in Haditha, came from human sources. Sparsely populated, Whiskey's AO required a novel approach to interdicting Al Qaeda's activities in the area. These activities notably included IED making and emplacement and the concealment of weapons and other materials that would later be used against Whiskey and the other companies. Whiskey's approach didn't involve berms, BATS, badges, or the IP but did involve a spreadsheet and a map in the hands of a second lieutenant, Dan Nidess.

Nidess, a field artillery officer trained as a forward observer, had joined the battalion in July, during 2/3's pre-deployment training at the Marine Corps Air Ground Combat Center at Twentynine Palms, California. Although it is standard to have an artillery officer as part of a Marine Corps weapons company, Nidess filled the role of company intelligence officer. His intel work would provide some of the most important intelligence gathered for the entire battalion.

While AQI hit Whiskey with 82mm and the powerful 120mm mortar attacks, sniper strikes, and small arms ambushes, IEDs proved the most vexing issue. Like all company intel officers, Nidess pored over daily intelligence reports pushed down from the battalion. These included intelligence data that came from both the battalion and RCT-7 and higher in the command chain in Iraq. These were helpful, particularly those regarding AQI strategic-level weapons caches. Nidess, analyzing one such report, led the company to a massive find of weapons, explosives, and other material buried near the Euphrates. Despite this and other similar successes, Nidess realized he needed to develop a system with which he could generate the company's own intelligence reports—not based on what he received from higher commands but based on data generated within the company itself.

Every day, Nidess studied imagery of Whiskey's AO on FalconView, a program that built maps using a variety of base data, including images captured by satellites and aircraft, digital elevation models, and aeronautical charts. Though powerful, FalconView fell short of the geospatial analysis capabilities of the world's most robust Geographic Information Systems (GIS) software. The most powerful GIS platforms can graphically illustrate trends and even provide predictive statistical analyses, for example, to help to determine where AQI will most likely deploy IEDs in the near future, and where in-place IEDs might most likely be found. Driven by the necessity of saving lives and limbs, the second lieutenant added the extra capability by combining FalconView with an Excel spreadsheet.

Using the two, Nidess plotted the site of every single IED the company had hit or located, down to the square meter. He also plotted locations of caches of weapons the company found, as well as other significant actions, including locations of mortar strikes, ambushes, and sniper strikes. FalconView provided a high-level graphical view, and Excel provided the details of each data point plotted on it, including type of IED and triggering mechanism. This analysis technique yielded "cluster sites" of areas where AQI had emplaced IEDs and where it had hidden components for making IEDs.

Armed with this intelligence, Whiskey began interdicting an increasing number of IEDs simply by scouring the cluster areas. The successes that the battalion realized in the core of the Triad may have forced AQI into the desert in and around Albu Hyatt, but the data analysis of their activity and subsequent actions based on this information began to slash most of Al Qaeda's remaining potency in the Albu Hyatt region. By late January, Weapons had racked up success after success in terms of discovering emplaced IEDs and weapons caches. Still, a few sharp teeth remained on the enemy.

WITH THE DRAMATIC calming of enemy activity in Haditha, Second Lieutenant Brian Park's platoon returned to Whiskey

Company from their attachment to Echo in the first week of 2007. By late January, with the security situation throughout the AO improving by the day, members of the battalion began to look forward to returning home. Gunnery Sergeant Terry Elliott, the platoon sergeant for Park's platoon, spoke with his wife Loretta every chance he could get to hear about her and their newborn son, Preston. Married out of high school, this would be the best reunion in the couple's life, one that would mark a new chapter in their lives as a family. Despite the homecoming on the horizon, he never wavered in his resolve or dedication to the mission or to the Marines under his watch. Everyone knew him to be a Marine who would never ask anyone to do a task or undertake a mission that he wouldn't.

"Sir!" Corporal Jason Schmus woke First Lieutenant Regan Turner from a quick nap. "Sir!"

"Yeah." Turner checked his watch as he sat upright: 3:15 in the morning on the first of February. Turner, a commander of one of Whiskey's platoons, had been standing by on QRF duty in an abandoned house in the desert west of Albu Hyatt.

"One of our patrols hit a catastrophic IED, sir," Schmus said. "The call just came in." Regan sprang to his feet and threw on his flak jacket and Kevlar helmet. "There's two urgent WIAs and two MIAs."

"MIAs?" Turner said. "What do you mean, MIA?"

"There's no sign of Doc Conte or Gunny Elliott, sir." Schmus paused. "They're missing in action."

Missing in action, Turner wondered. *They got thrown from the vehicle and the others in the platoon can't find them?* He could think of no other explanation.

Staff Sergeant Terry Southworth received the urgent medevac call at the Albu Hyatt FOB. He immediately routed the call to Al Asad as First Lieutenant Turner, Corporal Schmus, and others of the QRF sprinted out of the abandoned house. They felt the cold of the early morning winter air and felt the rhythmic gurgling of idling diesel engines of the convoy. Then they saw a yellow-orange glow surging into the sky in the western distance. They didn't need to reference a map. That glow marked the destination of their QRF, roughly three miles distant.

As a Dustoff lifted off from Al Asad and roared low over the desert, the QRF convoy sped into the open desert toward the site of the IED. The glow surged higher into the sky as the four-vehicle convoy closed in on what all would soon realize was a scene of total devastation.

A couple minutes later the tops of the flames that cast the glow flicked into view. The convoy crested a gentle hill, and the entire situation emerged before them just as the Dustoff flared and landed. The twisted, eviscerated carcass of an up-armored Humvee lay upside down, its ruptured fuel tank loosing the flames that lit the sky for miles. Chunks of hot metal, ripped from the vehicle in the explosion, smoldered in a debris field surrounding the burning hulk.

The QRF convoy halted. Turner and the others of the quick reaction force sprinted toward the site of the devastation. The engines of the Black Hawk spun into a scream. The helicopter lifted off with two Marines, each writhing in agony from burned flesh, smashed eardrums, splintered bones, and pummeled internal organs. "Where are Gunny Elliott and Doc Conte?" Lieutenant Turner asked a Marine of the stricken patrol.

"They're gone," the Marine answered.

"Gone?" Regan said. "Was there another Dustoff?"

"No. That was the only Dustoff," the Marine said.

Minutes earlier, the convoy in which Gunnery Sergeant Terry Elliott and Navy Hospital Corpsman Matthew "Doc" Conte rode had turned off MSR Bronze. The four-vic patrol had edged along the contour toward an overwatch point used frequently by tanks attached to the battalion. The lead seven-ton crawled through a broad draw, then began to ascend to the overwatch point. The second vehicle, a Humvee, followed moments later. Then the third vic, another Humvee, descended into the draw. The driver, Lance Corporal Terry Dunn, followed the tracks of the two lead vehicles closely. Gunny Elliott sat in the vehicle commander's seat, Doc Conte sat behind him, and Lance Corporal Jeremy Stengel manned the turret.

CLICK. The Humvee hit a pressure plate the first two vehicles had missed or for some reason hadn't depressed fully. The IED circuit closed. Electricity surged into a massive IED composed of artillery rounds and mines that AQI had emplaced to kill one of the Abrams tanks. The explosion had erupted directly under Gunny Elliott and Doc Conte.

"There was no other Dustoff, sir," the Marine repeated to Lieutenant Turner. "The explosion vaporized Gunny Elliott and Doc Conte."

The blast had thrown Stengel nearly fifty meters, shattering his left femur and right foot and shocking his internal organs. The driver, Terry Dunn, suffered third-degree burns over 80 percent of his body.

"We're just searching for pieces of Gunny and Doc at this point."

The Marines remained on scene for hours—well past sunrise—quietly filling body bags. Jason Schmus, who took the lead in recovering the remains of his two friends from the desert floor, thought of Doc Conte, Lance Corporal Dunn, and Stengel. Of course, he also thought of Gunny and his wife, Loretta—and their infant son, Preston. Born on the 231st birthday of the institution to which Gunnery Sergeant Terry Elliott had devoted so much of his life, he would never meet his father.

25

— ★ —

FLARE-UPS OF TRAGEDY
AMID A DYING FIRESTORM

HORRIFIC LOSSES—TWENTY-ONE MEMBERS OF 2/3 HAD FALLEN to AQI attacks by the beginning of February 2007. Yet both hard statistics and anecdotal evidence hinted that victory lay within reach of the battalion. Marines continued to discover weapons caches throughout Haditha, Barwana, Haqlaniyah, and Albu Hyatt. They detained one group of AQI personnel after another, many high ranking in the terror organization. AQI, on its knees, resorted to the most base of desperation tactics: hand grenades and suicide bombings.

On February 7, less than a week after the horrendous IED attack that took the lives of Gunny Elliott and Doc Conte, an AQI operative, dressed as an IP officer, nervously walked into an entry control point in Barwana. At the time, Fox Company had been working with the 2nd Battalion of the 4th Marine Regiment, the 15th Marine Expeditionary Unit's battalion landing team, or BLT.

That day, Fox Company Marines accompanied 2/4's Jump CP at the entry point. The Jump included Lieutenant Colonel James "Jim" Glynn, the commanding officer of 2/4, and Sergeant Major Joseph Ellis, the battalion's sergeant major.

While there, the members of the Jump observed one of the more critical components of the Marine Corps' COIN efforts employed throughout the Triad, Al Anbar, and all of Iraq: Lionesses. Out of cultural sensitivity, the Marine Corps relied on female Marines, not males, to search local women for weapons and other contraband at entry control points. The Lioness program trained female Marines not only for finding hidden explosives and weapons but also for combat. The Lioness program became essential to the overall war effort throughout Al Anbar. (Contrary to popular notions, female Marines—Lionesses—served in the very worst of combat theaters in Iraq side by side with their male counterparts.)

Sergeant Major Ellis, just weeks from retirement, noticed the nervous IP imposter and approached him. The man raised his hands in a surrender gesture. A cord extended from the man's wrist to his chest—a triggering mechanism. Sergeant Major Ellis rushed the man just as he fully extended his arms, triggering the suicide vest packed with machine screws and ball bearings. The explosion killed Ellis immediately.

By jumping toward the attacker, Ellis had saved Marines he placed behind him. As the dust cleared, more than a half dozen Iraqi civilians lay dead, and nearly as many Marines had been injured. One of the wounded, twenty-year-old Marine Corporal Jennifer Parcell, a Lioness, died of her wounds. She was the fifth female US Marine to die in Iraq.

CORPORAL TYLER HERMAN looked at his watch on Valentine's Day 2007. Thirty minutes remained of the six-hour patrol. A fire team leader in Golf Company, Herman scanned his surroundings. The complex character of Haqlaniyah seemed to reveal a new facet on each patrol the corporal undertook. A window he hadn't noticed before, the shape of a roof, the color of a door. He led his team into a small, two-story concrete building that sat next to a mosque. Inside, Herman joined Lieutenant Adam Steele, one of Golf's platoon commanders, and some of Herman's fellow Golf Company Marines, including Lance Corporal Travis Dodson and Lance Corporal Daniel Morris.

With the next patrol ready to head out, Herman removed his right boot. The crash of breaking glass snagged his attention. "GRENA—" BOOM! Herman walked into the adjoining room. Blood coated the floor. A hand grenade, thrown by an AQI operative from below, had landed in Travis Dodson's lap, then exploded. Next to Dodson, Morris lay on the floor. Herman heard nothing for a few seconds but dead silence. Then the room erupted with Marines trying to save the lives of both Dodson and Morris. Dodson vomited on the floor, moaning. A medevac spun up.

The Marines got the two wounded to the ground floor. Herman tightened a tourniquet on one of Morris's legs, but he saw no blood. He knew he had died. Before the Marines loaded Dodson, a good friend of Herman's, onto a Humvee to race him to the waiting Dustoff, Herman kissed the lance corporal on the cheek. "I love you, man," he said.

Despite the feverish attempts of corpsmen, Lance Corporal Daniel Morris died. Surgeons saved Dodson, although the blast necessitated amputating his left leg at his hip and his right leg below the knee.

Less than two weeks later, on the twenty-sixth of February, 2/3 lost its twenty-third member when Golf Company's Lance Corporal Anthony Aguirre stepped on a pressure-plate IED in Haqlaniyah during a sweep. The explosion killed him instantly. By that point in the deployment, like most others in the battalion, Aguirre had already begun making plans to see his family upon his return.

THE BATTALION WOULD not lose another member after Aguirre. As strong as the phantom enemy had proved to be, 2/3 consistently bested them.

But the deployment wasn't over yet, and neither was the fight.

26

★

COIN CULMINATION AND A CARAVAN

As THE DAYS GREW LONGER IN THE FINAL THROES OF WINTER IN Al Anbar, the mood grew inexorably brighter throughout the Triad. The last of the AQI operatives and sympathizers either fled or fell into the hands of the IP, attacks dwindled to next to nothing, and the battalion and its IP and Iraqi Army partners hauled in more hidden weapons and cached AQI supplies. The battalion actually saw a decline in weapons cache discoveries—because it had found most all of them. More importantly, the Iraqi Police and the Iraqi Army units increasingly conducted their own operations and patrols, repeatedly.

Furthermore, working with city leaders and Billy Parker and his CMOC, 2/3 helped find a mayor who would work with Farouk to maintain safety of the citizenry and foster municipal growth and economic vitality throughout Haditha and the whole Triad. Under the command of Colonel Clardy, RCT-2 supported the battalion's efforts to complete Trane McCloud's operational vision without hesitation or any friction whatsoever.

Engineers reinforced the berms, built the final entry control points and vehicle control points, and helped fully integrate the BATS system and badging, ensuring hostile elements couldn't get into the Triad while allowing free movement of the area's citizens and the continued flourishing of commerce.

The deployment had been a great lesson. No field manual, lecture, or textbook could have prescribed the multitude of initiatives that complemented each other to achieve the progress that 2/3 had made. Members of the battalion also recognized a common thread in their deployment: classic Marine Corps adaptability underlain by mission fidelity—cardinal institutional traits.

As far as they had come, Captain Tracy saw the job wasn't finished. The evolution of the area wasn't complete. Throughout, he had identified one final goal: enduring success. *Enduring* success meant that, once the Marines left, and once the battalion that followed them departed, the city of Haditha—and hence the entire Triad region—would never fall into the execrable state that they'd found it upon their arrival.

"CIVICS CLASS," CAPTAIN Tracy said to Billy Parker. "Civics class is super boring because you think you'll never need it. I'm seeing the necessity now, though. But what they teach in civics class comes in handy when you want to run a municipal government."

The IP in Haditha had steadily grown under Farouk's leadership and the battalion's oversight. "Peace is breaking out all over the city, all over the Triad. But we're at a point now, in this evolution, where we have to stop and question its legitimacy." Tracy pointed to the homogeny of the Iraqi Police force in Haditha. "They're all from Farouk's tribe, the Judaci," he said. "What we see as success might backslide into totalitarianism or an oligarchy."

Tracy recognized that they needed people of a variety of local tribes to participate in the police force and the city council.

Furthermore, from his months on the streets of the city, he understood that the key to obtaining the participation of men from all regional tribes hinged on the participation of one man, Sheik Barun. Barun, one of the most respected individuals in the entire area, had remained in the shadows for both AQI and the Americans. However, he was a leader. People listened to his proclamations, propagated through mosques and among individuals. With just weeks to spare before the turnover to 1/3, achieving backing from Sheik Barun became Tracy's main effort.

Captain Tracy had first met Sheik Barun months earlier, after the horrific IED incident north of Haditha that had killed and maimed a number of schoolchildren. Perhaps no other incident proved to the people of the area the intent and commitment of the Marines to the local populace and simultaneously highlighted the barbarism of AQI. Tracy met with Barun in late February, and then numerous times through early March, seeking his help and support.

"This isn't for me, the Marines, or for the Americans," he told the sheik. "This is for the people here, you, your family, your children," the captain emphasized.

The sheik finally agreed: he would support the movement, become part of the "Haditha Awakening," and speak with a number of men in his tribe to ask them to join the Iraqi Police in the city of Haditha.

But on March 10, with the first of 1/3's advance party arriving, events took a disastrous turn.

"UGH!" CAPTAIN TRACY screamed. In the makeshift weight room at the Haditha FOB with some Echo Marines, the company commander attempted to get his name on the "300 Club" wall by bench-pressing three hundred pounds. On his way to locking his arms, he felt a pop and a tear. The bar fell back onto his chest. One of the Marines jumped atop Tracy and wrestled the weights off him.

"UHHHHHHH!" he yelled. "Listen to me," he panted. "I'm screaming like a rabbit that a cat just caught!" A couple of Marines dragged Tracy into the base aid station.

"At a minimum, you tore your pectoralis muscle," Doc Oppliger told the captain. "I think you're going home early." The corpsman administered some morphine, then Tracy called Lieutenant Colonel Donnellan. Donnellan shook his head in disbelief.

"Well, it's better to do something stupid like this a few weeks before heading home than a few weeks after arriving," the battalion commander remarked.

"Sir," Ben Early said. He had run into the aid station and saw Tracy lying on his back, clutching his chest. "The IP just showed up. AQI got Sheik Barun. They got a guy to shoot him."

"Sheik Barun is dead?" Tracy asked. "I'm not hallucinating this, am I?"

"No. You aren't hallucinating," Early said. "They got him. He had a list of men who were going to sign up for the police. He was actually on his way here with the list when he got shot."

"Oh no," Tracy responded. "This was going to be it. We almost had it." He lay back and stared at the ceiling. "We almost had this."

As the captain drifted into a morphine-induced stupor, he pondered the long term. *What's a short-term victory worth? Nothing. We wanted the long term. I don't think we'll get it now.*

"MY FATHER IS dead!" Omar, Sheik Barun's eldest son, yelled to Captain Tracy a few hours later in the Echo FOB. "What are you going to do about this?" Omar, other men of Sheik Barun's family, and their wives and children had just arrived in Haditha to start new lives anchored by the men working for Farouk and the resurgent local Iraqi Police force.

"I'm in so much pain," Tracy responded, on his back. "I'm bedridden. I can't get dressed. I'm on painkillers and can't think straight. I can't hold a weapon." He paused. "I can't leave the FOB, but we'll get to the bottom of this. I think they're going to take me out of here, medevac me to Al Asad in a few hours for surgery. We don't even know what's wrong with me. There's been no formal diagnosis. It's out of my hands."

"You're pathetic!" Omar responded. "All these weeks, you show up to my father's home, begging for his help, challenging us to help you to bring peace. He finally helps you—and now he's dead and you're just a coward, hiding in this FOB. Cowering in your safe little FOB because you hurt your arm." Omar paused, then approached Tracy, looking him dead in the eye. "You promised me," he said. "And now my father is dead!"

Tracy pondered the situation in his drug-addled state. *Omar is right,* he realized. *Absolutely right.*

Then Donnellan called. Tracy assumed that he would be ordering him to Al Asad. "You're not going anywhere," the battalion commander said. "There won't be any medevac for you to Al Asad."

"You beat me to it," Tracy responded. "I was about to call you and request that I stay—that I finish out my weeks here." *Have to prove ourselves to the people,* the company commander repeated in his head.

Omar and twenty-five men and their families arrived at the Echo FOB the next morning. "So, we are leaving. All of us," Omar said. "It isn't safe here for our families." The twenty-five additional IP—men outside of Colonel Farouk's direct sphere— would prove to be the final, culminating factor in the COIN equation in the region.

"No," Tracy responded, in excruciating pain. "I'm staying, and we're going to get whoever did this to your father. I promise. Just give us a few days." Tracy knew that the IP and his Marines could protect the men and their families. He knew that AQI lacked the resources for any initiatives other than stabs at "lucky shots," like what he believed the assassination of Barun to be. But AQI needed to be lucky just one more time. The success of the campaign, Tracy believed, hinged on the next hours. *Could we find Barun's killer or killers? Could we convince Omar and his men to stay, to join the IP?*

"Early," Tracy called to his lieutenant. "Let's get some duct tape."

Ben Early duct-taped Tracy's left arm to his flak jacket, stabilizing his chest injury. An hour later, the company commander had assembled a squad of Echo Marines and Farouk and his IP.

"You don't have to do this, sir," Early said to Tracy. "You can barely move."

"Not being able to hold a weapon is kind of liberating," Tracy responded. "Besides, in pure COIN, who needs weapons?" He paused. "So long as you guys can open the door to the Humvee for me, then we'll be fine."

For ninety-six hours, the Marines and IP, under Tracy's command, scoured Haditha, searching for Sheik Barun's assassin. They returned to the Echo FOB with a few detainees, then crossed back outside the wire. Only a few dead-end leads emerged, however. Barun's killer evaded them.

The days-long attempt, however, convinced Omar and the other men of the fallen sheik's tribe. "We'll stay," Omar said. "We'll join the IP and even be on the city council." The pledge came with one condition.

"They'll join us," Tracy told Lieutenant Colonel Donnellan over a phone call. "All of them will remain in Haditha and work with Farouk."

"That's great," Donnellan responded.

"But there's one catch," Tracy said.

"Yeah—"

"We have to relocate their families to Al Qaim, up by the Syrian border," Tracy said. "The men believe in the mission, they believe in us, and most importantly, they believe in the IP and the resurgent city. But they know the history of Haditha, and they want their wives and children to remain safe."

"We're the Marine Corps," Donnellan answered. "Not a moving company." The risks of undertaking such a move would be incredible. Dozens of people and all of their possessions caravanning over seventy-five miles to the Syrian border would present opportunity after opportunity for any remaining shreds of Al Qaeda to attack the innocent families of the freshest members of Haditha's IP. Even moving a few miles outside the Triad would be incredibly dangerous—and this request was for a trip over dozens of miles of the wildest of the wild west of Iraq. Donnellan, however, knew the stakes well. "It's worth it," he decided. "Move them up there."

With just days remaining before the battalion's departure, Tracy and Ben Early quickly assembled a convoy. The caravan would include multiple seven-tons and Humvees loaded with food, water, and fuel to last days. The vehicles would carry the families of the IP and all of their possessions. They'd also carry a number of corpsmen, extra medical aid, and thousands of rounds of ammunition as well as spare weapons. To avoid IEDs, the convoy would traverse open desert. For extra protection, Marine F/A-18D Hornets and AV-8B II Harrier jets and Marine Corps UH-1N Hueys and AH-1W SuperCobra gunships would swap out providing cover. The convoy would be led by Lieutenant Ben Early and Sergeant Mike Dowling, and Tracy briefed the Marines and Navy Corpsmen of the mission on the morning of their departure. "Bring back a photograph of you guys right on the Syrian border after you safely deliver these families to their new homes in Al Qaim," he said.

Minutes after the caravan roared outside of the wire of Echo's FOB, Tracy met with Farouk. The IP leader had uncovered new information about the assassination of Barun. Later that night, with Tracy still writhing in pain from his injury, they launched a raid.

"They have him, sir," Marwan, Tracy's interpreter, reported to the company commander at three in the morning. "The IP captured him—and he's confessed to killing Sheik Barun."

Then the showdown came, much like the showdown at the beginning of the deployment that ended in Farouk beating an AQI leader to death with his bare hands.

"He's our prisoner," Farouk said. "We'll handle him."

"He needs to come back to the FOB for processing," Tracy responded. "And then he'll get sent through the judicial system."

"Judicial system!" Farouk yelled. "He's the one who killed Sheik Barun! We'll take him. He'll come with us. He's our prisoner!"

"Okay," Tracy acquiesced. The IP put the prisoner in the last vehicle of a convoy, an Iraqi Police truck. "Let's move," Tracy told his driver in the lead vic of the patrol. The convoy lurched forward. The captain thought about the deployment. He pondered the rules, the laws, the consequences, the reason he and the battalion deployed there, the talks he had given, his outlook. Still in excruciating pain, he thought about decision making under duress—while exhausted, while in pain. He thought about the ease of turning a blind eye with home so close. "Stop the convoy," Tracy said. "Where's that last IP truck?" The rear vehicle had fallen out of sight. Tracy ordered the convoy to double back. They found the truck on a side road. "We're taking the prisoner," Tracy ordered.

The IP accompanying Sheik Barun's killer glared at the captain.

"He's coming with us. We'll process him and he'll be dealt with according to the laws of your country."

27

★

COLORS AND CRYING

"Sergeant Dowling," Captain Tracy said. "You get that photograph of all of you on the Syrian border?" Tracy met the caravan upon its return a few days after the Marines and Navy Corpsmen successfully delivered the families of the new IP recruits to Al Qaim.

"Yes, sir," Dowling responded.

"And you guys didn't get shot at once?"

"Not one shot," the sergeant reported.

"Not one IED," Tracy said. "Nothing?"

"Not even a dirty look."

"Excellent," Tracy said.

"How's your injury?"

"Awful. It hurts like hell," Tracy said. "And I still don't know what's wrong with it."

THE PEACE THAT had bloomed and then burgeoned in Haditha and the entire Triad in December reached a crescendo by late

March. AQI had vanished, and unlike during other periods of the war in Iraq, it didn't resurface in another location. The Haditha Triad, and in particular the city of Haditha, had been its last stand—and the battalion had defeated it. They had defeated it directly and indirectly by working with the IP.

As the members of 2/3 planned to return home, Marines and attachments of 1/3 accompanied them on left seat, right seat familiarization patrols. 1/3's experience in the Triad would be very different from 2/3's. Instead of deserted byways and shuttered businesses, the streets throughout the Triad thrived. Marines bought and ate kabobs and ice cream from local vendors. They talked about sports, about plans for future businesses. The AQI shadow government long gone, people moved about freely, and "city works" of all types functioned regularly.

The Iraqi Police force had reached an effective and functioning level of operation. They developed their own operations and could execute them on their own. Furthermore, they developed their own robust operational tempo in the spirit of the Marines. They proved that they would never allow the region to again fall to groups like AQI.

The final days leading up to the official April 3, 2007, turnover of the AO to 1/3 were met with colors and crying locals. Each passing spring day seemed to bring more brilliance on the streets as parents allowed their sons and daughters, dressed not in black as AQI had mandated, but in colorful clothing, to emerge. A horrific chapter in the region's history had turned a bright corner.

With the new faces of the 1/3 Marines, the locals realized that those of 2/3 would soon depart. Residents, notably the IP and the mayor and his staff, swarmed members of the battalion, from the lowest ranks to Sergeant Major Wilkinson and Lieutenant Colonel Donnellan, crying. They begged them to stay—not out of fear of loss of protection but out of the spirit of friendship they'd built over the months of the Marines fighting and dying for their future. The population understood the immense sacrifices 2/3 had made on their behalf.

This remarkable transformation revealed itself not only anecdotally in Marines' personal observations but in raw numbers. In 2005, the 3rd Battalion of the 25th Marine Regiment lost forty-eight personnel in the Triad—the largest number lost by a Marine battalion in the war in Iraq, in all of the Global War on Terror, and since the 1983 Beirut bombings; 1/3 would lose *zero* throughout its deployment. History would record 1/3 as the only Marine battalion to record not a single KIA in the Iraq War. Throughout their tour, members of 1/3, of all ranks, regularly sent messages of gratitude to their predecessors. Instead of watching for mortars, rockets, snipers, and RPGs when leaving the confines of buildings in FOBs, they were able to watch outdoor movies with the locals of the city.

2/3's tour in the Triad—a culmination of Marine Corps efforts, notably those of 3/3—represented perhaps the greatest victory in the entire war in Iraq, and one of the greatest in the modern history of conflict. No other campaign or operation or battle demonstrated such an extreme, stark turn. Al Qaeda had been defeated, defeated in its final stronghold, destroyed months before the first of the lionized "Surge" of troops began arriving in Baghdad.

The numbers demonstrate this success, but the picture of this victory is best seen through the recollections of those who served in the Haditha Triad:

One of the things I'm most proud of in my entire life was the transformation of Haditha. When we got there, there was no market. Nobody was out. Women couldn't be seen in public without being accompanied by a man, and they had to wear all black and cover their face. At the end we couldn't go twenty-five feet down a street without someone pulling us into their store or house and feeding us. Women were free to be out alone or in groups of other women, and they could dress however they liked. There was color and life. We brought life to a city of death.

—JARED CAMPBELL

When we got there, it was hell. There was no law and order. Al Qaeda ruled the place. The people there lived in fear. When we left, the place was safer than most cities in the United States. The locals would run out and hug us on the streets. They'd bring us food and invite us inside. They started calling us the Angels of Anbar. The biggest takeaway of our success was that we risked everything to make sure the mission was accomplished, and the locals saw that.

—ANDREW FARLAINO

When I went back to Al Anbar in 2009 it was unbelievable. Oh my God, peace had broken out. It was such a victory. The Iraqis had held their own peace, business was coming in, infrastructure was being rebuilt. I wished my 3/3 guys could have seen it.

—WILLIAM STABLES, *Sergeant Major for 3/3 during its 2006 Haditha Triad Deployment*

NONE OF THE members of the battalion would ever forget the sacrifices made to achieve this victory. Twenty-three members of the battalion had died, and 177 had sustained serious wounds. The last Marines of 2/3 to leave the Triad arrived back at Marine Corps Base Hawaii at Kaneohe Bay on the eleventh of April 2007. Just over a week later, on the nineteenth, the battalion held its memorial service for the twenty-three fallen.

The memorial service marked the true end of their historic deployment, and as such, the beginning of a lifetime of reflection by all who participated in it. In subsequent months and years, the Marines of the deployment thought of friends made and lost. They thought of those changed forever by the good, the great, and the horrific. They would reminisce about daily life in the Triad, from burn shitters to Dustoff medevacs and eating Iraqi ice cream on once-deserted streets. They thought about weeks without a proper shower, picking up pieces of their best friends after a catastrophic IED strike, the view of the desert at sunset, dressing up as robots and then elves and handing out flyers spit from a decades-old ditto machine.

Brightest of all, however, each would remember leaving the AO in a far better state than they had found it. Memories of the colors of victory would endure the longest.

EPILOGUE

LEGACY

LOCATED ON THE CORNER OF 8TH AND I STREETS IN THE SOUTH-
east quadrant of Washington, DC, the Marine Barracks serves
as the home to the sitting Commandant of the Marine Corps.
Colloquially called "8th and I," the Barracks is the oldest and
most storied of the Marine Corps' installations. Each year, the
Marine Corps Association and Foundation hosts the Marine
Corps Association and Foundation Ground Awards Dinner,
where the Commandant presents the Leftwich Trophy for Out-
standing Leadership. Named in honor of US Marine Corps
Lieutenant Colonel William Leftwich, who was killed during a
combat operation in November 1970, the Leftwich is awarded
to a Marine captain who served as a ground commander in
combat. Chosen by the Commandant himself from a field of
nominations from the entire active component of the Marine
ground forces, this is the highest honor for a company-grade
ground combat leader, and one of the most important in all of
the Marine Corps. Only one is bestowed per year.

Among an incredibly strong field of candidates for the 2006
Leftwich, the Commandant of the Marine Corps, General James
T. Conway, chose Captain Matt Tracy to receive the award
based on his time as Echo Company commander in Haditha.

After shaking hands with the Commandant and receiving the trophy, Tracy stood at the lectern and discussed the efforts of the Marines of Echo Company under his command, thrilling all in the audience with stories of incredible bravery and sacrifice.

Also in the audience was Colonel Blake Crowe, the former commander of RCT-7, who in the past had been a source of frustration for Tracy.

Captain Tracy wasn't the only member of 2/3 to whom General Conway presented an award. Nominated by Sergeant Major Patrick Wilkinson and Lieutenant Colonel Jim Donnellan, James Steuter, one of Tracy's Echo Company Marines, won the 3rd Marine Division Marine of the Year award. "There were so many great Marines throughout the battalion," Wilkinson said. "Steuter was one of the best we had."

BUT AWARDS REPRESENT just a small part of the legacy of the Triad deployment for members of 2/3. Some Marines and officers, finishing out their contracts, retired in the months and years following the deployment. They then struck off in different directions to pursue new opportunities. One manages an organic beef cattle ranch. A number became lawyers. Some became doctors. A few became scientists. Some work in law enforcement. A number started their own businesses. At least one became a professional triathlete, and a handful, who suffered amputations, became Olympians.

None, however, forget. Regan Turner visits Gunny Elliott's widow and her and Terry's son, Preston, regularly. Many get together every year or every few years to speak about topics nobody but them can grasp—at least not in the way they can. To virtually all of the battalion, the deployment represented the most important, most salient, most intensely memorable experiences of each of their lives.

The rise of ISIS grabbed the attention of all who served with 2/3 in the Triad. Although the Islamic State took control of roughly 75 percent of Al Anbar Province, it never took the Triad, including the Haditha Dam, one of its stated targets.

"I'd like to think that the IP and Iraqi Army forces we trained and worked with were the ones that repulsed them," Adam Steele said. "I can't think of any other reason that ISIS couldn't have taken control."

"To my knowledge, Haditha was one of the only cities in western Iraq that did not fall to ISIS," Victor Lance said. "I believe Farouk is still the police chief to this day. I feel a great sense of pride in knowing that the guy we went and found in northern Iraq was in fact the right man for the job."

WITHIN THE MARINE Corps, the legacy of the historic deployment remains strong. Matt Tracy, who is still in the Marine Corps to this day, rose steadily in rank, always remembering the sacrifices of all those of the battalion. As a Lieutenant Colonel, Tracy became the commanding officer of 3/3, a job once held by Norm Cooling (now a general). Before work each morning as the commanding officer of 3/3, Tracy would stop in front of Mackie Hall, a barracks that has served as home for generations of infantry Marines throughout all three battalions of the 3rd Marine Regiment—Marines like Mike Scholl, Jeremy Sandvick Monroe, and many others of 2/3. One day, as he sat on the hood of his car and watched the Marines of Mackie begin their day, a sergeant working at a neighboring building approached him.

"Sir," the Marine said.

"Yes," Tracy responded.

"Sir, I see you out here every morning. Just staring up at Mackie. What are you doing?"

"I'm listening," Tracy responded.

"Listening? Who are you listening to?"

"I'm listening to ghosts, sergeant."

"Ghosts?" the Marine asked. "Ghosts?"

"Yeah, sergeant," Tracy said. "Ghosts."

"What are they saying?" the sergeant asked after a pause.

"They're saying 'don't ever forget us.'" The sergeant stared at Tracy. "And then sometimes they speak Latin."

"Latin?" the sergeant asked. "What do they say in Latin?"

Lieutenant Colonel Tracy smiled at the sergeant.

"They say Semper Fidelis."

SOURCES

THE PRIMARY RESEARCH FOR THIS BOOK BEGAN IN EARLY 2007 when I embedded with 2/3 in the Haditha Triad region (this followed my embed with the battalion in September–October 2005 in Afghanistan). Lieutenant Colonel Jim Donnellan and his staff arranged for me to visit each company: Headquarters & Services, Company E, Company F, Company G, and Whiskey Company. During my time with the battalion, both inside and outside the wire, I gained an appreciation for their deployment that would have proven unachievable by any other means. Although a book on the battalion's time in the Triad was a long way off at that point, my experiences laid a solid foundation from which to craft the narrative years later. Most importantly, having spent time on the ground with 2/3 opened doors with the members of the battalion—opportunities that in large measure would likely not have availed themselves otherwise.

To write their story, I conducted hundreds of interviews over a six-month period in 2018. In all, I interviewed more than sixty individuals (many multiple times) and transcribed more than 250,000 words of notes. The vast majority of the information for this book came from direct interviews of those listed below. This information from interviews was complemented by the battalion's command chronology documents (chronological timelines of events throughout the deployment), after-action reports, summaries of action reports, and three previously published works:

1. Norman L. Cooling and Roger Turner, *Understanding the Few Good Men: An Analysis of Marine Corps Service Culture*, http://www.darack.com/sawtalosar/USMC -SERVICE-CULTURE.pdf. *Understanding the Few Good Men* is, in my opinion, the best written work for an introduction to the Marine Corps. This was originally a paper for the Naval War College and it was published in 2007 on the DTIC.mil site (Defense Technical Information Center) by then Lieutenant Colonel Norm Cooling and then Lieutenant Colonel Roger Turner (as of the publication of this book, both are brigadier generals). The paper no longer is hosted on the DTIC.mil site. I republished *Understanding the Few Good Men* on my official website, Darack .com, on June 1, 2009. It has been used and cited dozens of times in books, magazine articles, and professional papers since then. I cannot recommend *Understanding the Few Good Men* strongly enough. In addition to Darack .com, the work is permanently archived here: https:// web.archive.org/web/20120105100757/http://www .darack.com/sawtalosar/USMC-SERVICE-CULTURE.pdf.
2. Ed Darack, *Victory Point* (New York: Penguin, 2009).
3. Ed Darack and Major Matthew Tracy, "Kilcullen's Principles in Action: Miracle in Anbar," *Marine Corps Gazette,* October 2007, 61–63.

I shot all the photographs used in the book during my embed with the battalion with Nikon F6 film cameras and Nikkor lenses using Fujichrome Velvia film, and then scanned them on a high-resolution scanner, with subsequent adjustments and corrections made using Adobe Photoshop software. The maps in this book were created by me using Adobe Illustrator software. They are based on US government remotely sensed base imagery and US government maps.

I conducted interviews with the following individuals:

Mario Anes-Menchaca
Steve Bolz
William Burke
Mike Cabrera
Josh Caddell
Jared Campbell
Pete Capuzzi
Dan Carroll
Eric Ciotola
Norman Cooling
Leonel Cuellar
Lance Davis
Dhurgham (Joe)
James Donnellan
Mike Dowling
Max Draper
Zackeri Drill
Ben Early
Keith Eggers
Andrew Farlaino
Dennis Gilbert
Doug Glover
Daniel Goldberg
Mike Greiger
Ron Gridley
Brian Guzzo
Tyler Herman
Dustin Hoppenjan
Jacob Kareus
Patrick Kinser
Thomas Kisch
JJ Konstant

Jared Kreiser
Victor Lance
Rob Long
Andrew Lynch
Jason Mattson
Festus McDonough
Tin Nguyen
Andrew Niccum
Dan Nidess
Philip Oppliger
Brian Park
Mark Perna
Aaron Rankin
Dan Renshaw
Justin Roudebush
Joe Roy
Jason Schmus
Rob Scott
William Stables
Adam Steele
James Steuter
Jim Sweeney
Jason Tarr
Matt Tracy
Regan Turner
Perry Waters
Elliott Weeks
Patrick Wilkinson
Travis Zabroski
Unnamed / Anonymous
Unnamed / Anonymous
Unnamed / Anonymous

INDEX

235